THE

Acknowledge Your Feelings

Honest Mom

Break Free From Expectations

PROJECT

Build Your Beautiful Life as a Mother

♡ You & all you've given me to make this book happen!! Michelle Mansfield

MICHELLE MANSFIELD

HOST OF "THE HONEST MOM PODCAST"

*To my daughter, Brooklyn, who has been
on this shit storm with me the entire time
and taught me so much about what it
truly means to be her mother.*

THE Honest Mom PROJECT

CONTENTS

INTRODUCTION

To the Mother Reading This Book,

I see you sitting in the corner with your latte and stroller. Looks like this may be your first adventure out of your house with your new baby. She's all cuddled in her stroller, dressed in the onesie from grandma, along with a beautiful rose blanket with a satin trim from your baby shower. Her eyes are closed peacefully as she sleeps. It's easy to look at this scene as an outsider and smile for you. Even with the soft filter and calmness that comes from you, I know this is one of the shortest periods of your day. I hope you're enjoying it because when you walk in that door of your house, you're back. It's not a happy "Honey I'm home!" feeling where you are excited and feel welcomed. Most of the time you dread coming home and going right back to where you were thirty minutes ago. The place you were escaping.

You don't know what else to do with her right now. Sitting in your home seems to be the easiest option. Perhaps it's winter, or maybe it's a hundred degrees out, gathering the items for the diaper bag is overwhelming, you wonder if she'll need to be fed (AGAIN), what if she cries, what if she has a diaper blow out, what if you run into someone, and the excuses build up. Most days you toss in the towel and say "F it!" to sit back down on the couch with her. She's nursing round the clock anyways so perhaps this is just temporary, and you should be staying at home.

You're probably saying, "Well, it's not like I'm TOTALLY alone right now; we've had a lot of visitors since we got home." I, too, had many people that dropped by after my daughter was born, reached out to see how she was doing, some even brought a meal or even offered to pick up my house. But the visits will stop. The reach outs and "need anything?" texts will be fewer. You're not reaching out either; you don't want to bother anyone or make anyone notice that you are drowning. With as much help as your mom has been, you even feel you're asking too much from her. You're a perfectionist on top of it, and so hard on yourself if you can't figure it out on your own. This is not something you're going to fail at, even if you're on Dr. Google at 3 a.m. overanalyzing the fifteen different pieces of advice on why she won't latch. To you, asking for help means you are failing. Where is this "mommy instinct" they talk about anyways?

But if you're on a deserted island with no compass, how are you supposed to find this?

Not only are you insecure about this mommy gig, but you haven't been taking care of yourself either. You feel guilty for even thinking about spending time with friends or leaving your baby for ten minutes to take a shower. You honestly get drained from just thinking about putting on makeup and blow-drying your hair—or even simply washing it.

When someone mentions the weekly date-nights they have, your head spins at what you and your partner would even do, who would watch the baby, how much milk would you have to pump, how much formula to make, the pain-in-the-ass pumping when you get home, your boobs leaking at the dinner table, your mind is distracted by wondering if the baby is crying, is she sleeping, why haven't I heard from my mother-in-law, my mother-in-law won't stop texting me, I'm not even enjoying this glass of champagne, is my partner even attracted to me right now, is he bored, we have nothing to talk to, we are both exhausted; OH MY GOD make it stop!

I know, I always wondered if it would even be worth it as well. So, we didn't have a date night for a long time. We survived and are still married.

I see you sitting in the corner. My friend, although no one is here to save you, I am here with my hand reaching out. To be by your side, make you feel normal, included, ease the guilt a tad, help you simply admit your feelings, and most importantly for you to know you're an incredible mother. You see, as I look at you, I'm also looking in a mirror and remembering things that I've gone through. I haven't forgotten how hard it can be and what my life was like that first year. Or second. Or even third. I, too, hid it from the ones that love and care about me. The ones that wanted to help and extend their hand to me from across the room. I will tell you this, no one will put you in the corner other than yourself. There are times when we can get our ass up and step out on the dance floor, but let's be honest, there are times when we need supportive and empathetic moms to drag us out there too. There's nothing wrong with how you get there as long as you get there and start dancing.

It's time to start your own Honest Mom Project.

With Love,
Michelle

CHAPTER 1

If I Could Turn
Back Time

I lay on my bed in my college apartment just a few days after I had graduated. I couldn't stop crying. More like sobbing. I called my college boyfriend to come over as I sat in my apartment alone and scared to death. When he arrived, I couldn't explain what was going on. All I could do was cry. When he left a few hours later, I was still in the exact same spot where I was when he arrived. After that, I naturally I called my mom. "I don't know what's wrong with me, Mom. I just can't stop crying. I feel so overwhelmed, and I don't know what to do."

Life was changing after I received that diploma. A big reality was staring at me in the face: MY NEW LIFE. It was time to let go of those four years of fun, freedom, friendships, and little responsibility. Not only did I make some of the best memories I've ever had, but I also had an amazing group of friends to say goodbye to as I packed my boxes for the last time. I didn't have a job yet. What made matters worse is I had this degree, $75,000 in school loans, and didn't know what I even wanted to do in life. There weren't any courses in "Adulting." I felt unprepared, insecure, and terrified.

Even though I knew I had my mother's support and a place to go back to, what was I going to do once I was there? What if I didn't want to go back?

Flash-forward and my panic eventually subsided, I found a job, and saved enough money to make the big move to Chicago. I gallivanted around in the bright lights, big city life, proudly wearing the "I'm NEVER Moving Back to the Suburbs!" badge. Living in the city was a time that I cherish to this day, and for some reason, I didn't have a difficult time adjusting to. Perhaps it was because I was escaping the stigma of living with my parents, again, and I was already one foot in the door to having a life of excitement back. I had my Mary Tyler Moore feels of making it, doing it on my own, and having a lot of fun and freedom at the same time. I had a consistent career, lived with my best friends, worked hard, played hard, and had no heavy responsibilities other than paying my rent, going to work, and making sure the electricity was paid for. Life was easy, but it was about to change and get complicated again.

Adjusting to a completely new way of life is HARD

I hesitated even being set up with my husband for just ONE specific reason. My best friend and her husband were the culprits (I mean cupids) and the only two people on the planet that didn't try to set me up with someone. So, I was curious. I trusted them and hoped it was better than all the other set-ups and online crap I was finding. What's crazy is when they listed off his first two "credentials," they winced, and to their surprise and mine, the first two didn't scare me. He was divorced. Eh, who isn't nowadays? They then told me he had two kids. Actually, that was pretty darn attractive to me coming from dating men that acted like children themselves. I was ready for a grown ass man with some sort of plan in life. What sent me over the edge was the third credential: He lived in the SUBURBS. Not just any suburb, but in a galaxy far, far away from the city. After some convincing,

I took a chance. Not taking any date too seriously, I figured it was simply a date, and it didn't mean I had to marry the guy. Well wouldn't you know, I started to believe in miracles. The first one is, love at first site does exist. The second miracle you ask? Six months later, I moved my ass to the suburbs.

Moving to the 'burbs, adjusting, and getting to know his children led us to wait about five years before even thinking of getting pregnant. So even though I was in the suburban family-zone, and the adjustment was difficult; it was still an autonomous life. My husband had 50/50 custody with his ex and my busy career and friends kept me connected to my past life in the city. During this time, we traveled a lot, bought a timeshare in Cabo San Lucas, went out to dinner often, sat in movie theaters watching grown-up movies, lounged on the couch binge watching Netflix, slept past 6 a.m., took Starbucks walks without a stroller, went to concerts past 10 p.m., and simply spent time together as husband and wife.

Was I ready for the biggest change yet?

I found out I was pregnant on Father's Day. Could it get any cheesier than that? Ironically, I was by myself as my husband was on the road with his son driving to a baseball tournament. It felt a bit off to tell him on the phone, but I knew I didn't want to wait until he got back. Obviously telling him on Father's Day was too perfect to pass up. Yes, I was excited, but there was also the strangest feeling inside of me. Even though I connected to the fact that I was going to have a baby, there was still this "it's just me" feeling that continued up until the day she was born. My pregnancy was beyond easy, and for a while, there really wasn't any evidence that had me truly believing I was about to become a mother. When my belly popped a few months later, and then eventually expanded, I *still* wasn't in Mom Mode. Probably because I'm typically a "deal with it when the shit hits the fan" type of person and tend to be disconnected until I absolutely have to. This whole Mom role just didn't seem real yet. But shit was about to get as real as it can get.

Nothing prepares you with how you will feel after your baby is born.

Nor can you fully prepare, predict, or even guess what it will truly be like. Sure, there are plenty of movies, television shows, reality shows, books, doctor appointments, and even some funny stories from friends and family, but the true reality is different for every mother. We all have our own interpretations, beliefs, feelings, reactions, chemical makeup, and history that create our own experiences. I won't say that my friends' stories, mother's advice, or a paragraph in one of the thirty "What to Expect" baby books didn't influence me in some way. My husband was in the "been there, done that" club, having already raised two children where he had some incredible tips and tricks that had me saying, "How the fuck did you know that?!" I could collect advice, tips, and tricks about my baby until I was blue in the face. THAT was something I could handle and felt I could somewhat prepare for. My baby. What I wasn't prepared for was how my own world would change and how I would *feel* about my new role as a mother. I didn't even *think* about how my own world was going to change and how incredibly challenging it would be. I was never warned that I was going from a life of 100 percent me to 99 percent my baby. No one gave me a head's up that during a simple trip of getting diapers at Buy Buy Baby, and a much-needed breather, that I would be getting texts from my husband at 10:15 a.m., saying, "She's hungry." Then at 10:17a.m., "She's starting to cry." Then at 10:20a.m. "She's crying really hard." I wasn't told I'd then be panicking in the car, tears streaming down my face, pissed at the world because I couldn't get there any faster. I didn't get the memo that at the stop light, I would scream out loud, "What the **FUCK** have I done?!"

Where is the life you loved, and what is this life have you been thrown into?!

I will admit, I had a bit more time to get a little too comfortable in the land of "Me" before my daughter was born. I'm probably considered an "old mom" in today's standards. Living in the city, on my own, working on my career, and doing what I wanted, when I wanted was my normal. There was nobody to answer to but my landlord, my boss, and ME. My free time was filled with relaxing on the couch on a Sunday watching movies or *Sex and the City*, traveling with girlfriends, staying out late, and sleeping in later. I'd grab coffee on a Saturday at the local coffee shop, find a comfy couch, and read the paper … alone. Taking a walk on the shore of Lake Michigan on a whim didn't require an "Is it OK if I …?" At times I'd bring a book on that walk, stop to sit in the grass, and read without interruptions. Perhaps even nap. I'd come home late at night and play my favorite music so loudly my neighbor would knock on the wall. I could make a last-minute decision to work out and not have to arrange childcare. TGIF meant something, and the weekends were cherished. All this sounds a bit self-centered, but this was the time in my life when I could do what they call "selfish things" with NO GUILT. This was the time I didn't have to check with my husband to see if it was "OK" for me to meet up with girlfriends for a drink (never has my husband said "no" by the way.) I didn't have to rush home, feel guilty for being gone too long, feel selfish for leaving her for a night or weekend with my husband or parents, or check in to make sure everything wasn't blowing up.

What's really going on, Mom?

I diagnosed myself with being nostalgic with all these changes in my life, to include the adjustment as a new mom. However, there's a big differ-ence between being nostalgic where you talk about the "good times" ver-sus holding onto the past to where it paralyzes you. Nostalgia can be a very healthy emotion that can benefit not only your present but also your future. "Nostalgia is the warm, fuzzy emotion that we feel when we think about fond memories of the past. It often feels bittersweet—mostly happy and comforting but with a tinge of sadness that whatever we're remembering is lost in some way." (Erica Hepper, Ph.D., a lecturer in the School of Psychology at the University of Surrey in England in an interview by *Huffington Post*.) Nostalgia can positively connect you to your past, people of your past, and learn from your past to create an even better future. As moms, I believe we are more sensitive to this, as we have a heightened awareness of how quickly life can change. However, the other side of living in the past can keep you stuck and prevent you from finding the life you should be living RIGHT NOW. The life you deserve. Even though I warmly reminisce about certain events and people of my past, there have been times where certain changes brought on debilitating anxiety inside of me because of my fear of the future and how I would handle it. If nostalgia is supposed to feel all "warm and fuzzy," why did I seem to have a nervous breakdown and latch on to the past when a big change was in front of me? It was safer and comforting for me to long for what *was* rather than *what could be*. It was invulnerable to go back to a life that was established, somewhat predictable, and a life I had pride and confidence in. When I became a mother, I basically went into a mourning state of my past life, disconnected from my present, which prevented me from moving toward the future. I never had a funeral or any sort of closure to be able to say goodbye to that life and recognize that I was in an entirely new one. As a new mom, why couldn't I let go and be vulnerable so I could welcome this new life in front of me? This wasn't nostalgia, and something bigger was going on.

I was recently asked about my difficult journey into motherhood,

"Oh yes I had huge regrets about having a baby. There were TOO many changes going on. Not only was my body torn up, burning, squirting, sore, floppy, and just exhausted ALL the damn time, but also, I had let go

9

of so many things. I missed all the fun and exciting things that I couldn't do anymore and was sad wondering if I ever would again. I felt like the world around me didn't change at all, but here I was being thrown into a new life that I couldn't escape. Gone were the water cooler conversations at work, lunch dates, drinks after work, dinners with clients, meeting friends out for a cocktail, weekend trips, vacations with my husband, concerts, plays, errands with no rush to get home, reading in the morning without looking at a baby monitor, and just doing things when I wanted to versus fitting them in with panic. I honestly felt these things defined me, and I was lost knowing that I could possibly never do them again. There was no definition of time when it came to doing the things I loved. I feared that these things would never be a part of my life and that I would have to create an entirely different person as a mom. I never felt more boring, insecure, and lost. The scary thing was, I couldn't return this new life for what I used to have. The even scarier part? I didn't even know what I truly wanted for my life."

What you're searching for

Feeling safe and secure about your future is a basic human need that is probably amplified when you become a mother. It's a natural human behavior to avoid pain and to seek things that will give you pleasure. If we want to get technical here, the safest and most secure state to live in is a life *without change.* I'm sure you will agree though, it's an impossible way to live. If change is bound to happen, how are we as mothers navigating through this huge change into motherhood? And at the same time, feeling safe and secure about our new life? This desire can motivate us to figure out our new world with excitement, but it can also create situations where you end up altering your life to avoid anything new coming into it. Let's figure out how you can welcome this change and figure out your own expectations, desires, and dreams so you can be certain that this is the life you're meant to live.

We are on the same team

Like you, I've had financial stress, moved, changed jobs, lost loved ones, and I will stand by this statement until the day I die:

BECOMING A MOTHER IS THE BIGGEST AND MOST DIFFICULT CHANGE I'VE EVER EXPERIENCED.

It is time that we as mothers acknowledge this feeling, honor it, and figure out how to work through it. For some reason, there are still people out there that make you feel uncomfortable to even think this way. When I was doing research for this book, I decided to do an online survey, asking moms about the challenges of letting go of their past life when they became a mother. There was an outpour of responses about all the time periods, events, trips, careers, and freedom that they missed. But as you can imagine, there are the gems that pop in with "I don't have ANY regrets; I love my life!" along with "You have nine months to prepare for motherhood, so it shouldn't be a big shock," or the best one was, "Motherhood is a choice, and you chose this life." First, if these women don't have ONE thing that they miss from their past life, then I truly feel they either lived in seclusion on top of a mountain or they are lying. Or if you truly didn't have a hard time adjusting, there's nothing wrong with that either. Live by my mom's philosophy instead. There are times when you need to be the mother-in-law at your son's wedding. You just "Show up, shut up, and wear beige." The judgmental tone versus sympathy for us mothers who are struggling is the exact reason these mom divisions and battles even begin.

Let's also face the facts. Like me, you miss your past life because it was a lot more fun than the one you're sitting in now. You're not selfish for admitting this nor are you a bad mother because of it. We as new moms are hypnotized by everything and everyone telling us how grateful we should feel, how blissful motherhood is, how it's changed someone's life completely (in a good way), how a baby "completes" them and they NOW know what their purpose is (I'm clapping for them, but it's not everyone's reality), and how it's the BEST thing that's ever happened to them. There are staged photos, edited stories, perfect family vacations, a family hugging with smiles and laughter, and a mom painting the town red as if nothing has changed. The reality of motherhood isn't the most marketable, so why would anyone feel comfortable telling the real story? As a result, we are afraid to be honest with how motherhood can really be.

Someone failed to mention ...

1. I wouldn't immediately enjoy being a mother.
2. I would have to say goodbye to so many things.
3. That I would miss these things as much as I did.
4. I'd have regrets about becoming a mother.
5. Not everyone feels the same way that I do.
6. But there are so many that do.

Changing your expectations

A challenge I see for new mothers, and I experience this myself, is avoiding the reality of the new life and new role we have when we become a mother. We first need to end the shame and acknowledge that becoming a mother, whether it's the first time or fourth, is a fucking hard change and takes time to adjust to. Maybe years. You need to find courage admitting that at times you may feel regret, nostalgia, frustration, and there may be days where you don't want to be in the chaos you're in.

For some reason, the outside world feels it's their duty to tell us we should be *grateful* and *happy* to be mothers. "WHO SAYS WE AREN'T?!" is what I want to shout back at the world and all the people that think they need to tell us how to feel. These outside voices, whether they come from your mother, friend, book, podcast, colleague, or a social media post, need to be blocked from entering your brain. Get that filter out, my friend! Sitting in your unique spot, finding those feelings, acknowledging them, and talking to them with someone you trust, is what will fuel your soul to figure out how these changes can fit into your life. Never push them under the rug. Just because one person tells you she didn't feel that way, that doesn't mean you're a bad mother or your feelings aren't real. They exist and are alive, and you need to take care of them.

Perhaps your career is still an important part of your life. If traveling with your friends was an important part of your life, that doesn't mean you're selfish. Your lazy Sundays on the couch with zero interruptions were heavenly, and no one can argue with that. What's awesome is you'll either get these things back eventually, or you may not want them at all in the future. Remember that you already had these experiences, so what's awesome is you already know how to get to them back once things die down a bit. It's perfectly OK to put them on a bookshelf while you focus on the human you are raising.

If it gives you anxiety simply thinking about fitting in something you used to do, honor this season in your life and that it may just be the wrong season for it. This season of your life is unique, so honor it and nurture it, versus holding on to something just because it was part of your past. Remember, you may not be saying goodbye to certain things completely, you're simply saying "Until the next time, my friend."

Let's break the patterns that are holding you back

1. As you're adjusting to your new life as a mom, do you find yourself constantly going back to your past life? If you are, the question you need to ask yourself is, "Am I letting these feelings hold me back from moving toward my future?"

2. As a mom, try to avoid using the word "never" too much. Most of the time you bite your tongue, and it makes it even harder to adjust to changes.

3. Expectations are bound to disappoint you and keep taking you further from joy. Just roll without expectations as much as you can and pay attention so you can appreciate how the day naturally unfolds.

4. Connect with the things that you miss and be honest if they are going to work in this season of life you're in. It doesn't mean you have to say goodbye to it forever, just put it on the shelf for when it's a better time for it.

5. On the same subject, connect with the things you miss and be honest if you even want to do them anymore! For me, I can't drink until 2 a.m., dance on tables, and flash people anymore. But more importantly, I don't want to!

6. Dig deep to find the awareness that this is an entirely new life you've been given. It should be honored, not avoided. Admitting that your life has changed and talking about it with others that understand will allow you to connect with your new life. Like all the other changes in your life, you will eventually find ways to embrace it and be proud of it. It just takes time so be patient, aware, and know it's OK to relax and change your expectations in order to find your happiness.

At the end of the day

Listen, it's perfectly normal and SANE to tell people that you LOVED that time in your life. It's not self-centered or ungrateful. It's OK to tell people that you MISS it at times. Be proud that you had an amazing time before you had a baby. Whatever you accomplished, the memories you built, the laughs, culture, exposure, growth, strength, and creativity you created should all be CHERISHED. These years have shaped you into a strong woman and hopefully the confidence to match that strength. The years and experiences before you became a mother have all prepared you for the mother you are meant to be.

Let's make you feel even better with something that took me years to believe. It's absolutely healthy to admit that you wish you had some of those things back. Maybe you don't want all of them back, but you can say it out loud and remember that you should never feel guilty for admitting it. There are some roadblocks that you'll need to get through which can only be conquered with acknowledging what's going on and talking about it with others. And remember to be prepared for different responses. These people will tell you their experiences, interpretations, meanings, and stories that literally have nothing to do with your life up to this point and beyond. I had to actively learn and try hard to listen with intention, process it all, then filter it all so I could figure out what I connected with.

This is an exciting new story for you, and you have the pen and power to create your own unique life. You have to believe this and commit to taking action toward this every day of your life. Don't run from it; this will only take you further from the joy that awaits you. Don't hide your feelings; this will only take you further from your healing. Be proud of your past but remember to connect to what is going on RIGHT NOW in this moment, so you can be the creator of your future as a mother.

CHAPTER 2

Your Identity Doesn't
Have to Be a Crisis

Before becoming a mother, I didn't realize how many things would change, how instantaneous the changes would be, and how hard they would be for my soul. There was zero preparation for the reality of where my life was headed and how to adjust to it. To this day, I don't know of a class, therapist, coach, or doctor who has a strategy to prepare a woman for the extreme changes she's about to experience when she steps into the role of "Mom."

Oh, I've been through some big changes in my grown-up world and had a hard time adjusting to my new life and new version of me. What I thought defined me.

The first night when I moved from Chicago into my husband's cookie-cutter, beige, suburban townhome was harder than my first night at away camp. I was living fifty miles from where I swore I'd never leave and unpacking boxes in the exact place that I proclaimed I'd NEVER be. I lived within rows of townhomes; each looked the same as the next; a cornfield was in spitting distance, along with a water tower, some power lines, and a Home Depot down the street. I know it sounds crazy, but living in the city was a huge part of my identity. For me, it meant I was hip, in the know, exciting, well-rounded, stylish, modern, cultured, and if you were a mom, you were all those adjectives along with the word "mom" behind it.

It didn't help that I also had a slew of my city friends reinforcing this idea that life is over once you move to suburbia: "Oh I'll never move to the suburbs; KILL ME if I ever do!", "I'm definitely raising my kids in the city; I'm not sheltering them in suburbia.", "The suburbs are so boring, and look what happens to you when you move there!", "There's no culture," "There's no diversity." We were a bunch of twenty-something-year-old girls with zero children, too many cocktails, and all the answers. We were already putting huge pressure and restrictions on ourselves, which created the suffocating identity that didn't allow breath or movement.

I felt like I was handing in my resignation

As I commuted from the suburbs to the city, I thought I would be able to handle being a working mom and had always planned on making it work. However, I was quickly hit in the face within the first week of having Brooklyn home.

I knew my career before entering that hospital was impossible for me to continue as a new mother. My current job wasn't the most "mom-friendly"; it didn't have a work-from-home option, nor was I mentally in a place to send out resumes or put on my control top pantyhose for interviews. During my maternity leave, I would pace around my dark home at all hours of the night, practicing the "Five S's" as Brooklyn screamed, and I struggled with breastfeeding. Sometimes she'd still be crying when my alarm would normally go off for work at 4:30 a.m.

As I looked out of one of our bedroom windows at the insane snowstorm blowing violently, I thought, "How the fuck am I going to make this all work?!" Other thoughts that crept in my mind included, "What am I going to do with my life now?" "What will I say to my boss? Will he think I'm weak?" "Do I really want to be a SAHM?" "What if I am not working for long enough where I can never return to this industry? What will I do then?"

Those thoughts traveled through my brain in a matter of thirty seconds as I looked out the window, tears welled up in my eyes as the blizzard in front of me got even stronger.

I had worked hard for this career, had been very successful, and was proud of the woman I was in this role: independent, fierce, valued, smart, and driven. I had a purpose. I could financially support myself. I had worth.

Was I also letting go of the "Fun Michelle"?

I had also always been the "social butterfly" and enjoyed being with interesting people, going to interesting places, and was up to date on all the "hot spots." I always had plans, laughing was always part of the night, and storytelling was my skill. Friends from every arena were around me as we painted our town, and any others, bright red.

Sitting on the reclining couch day in and day out, breastfeeding around the clock with barely any time to shower, put a bit of a damper on my social life to say the least. Not only was my body physically healing, but I was also had an emotional episiotomy. As a new mom, I'm sure you can relate to how in the beginning, it's impossible to think about hitting the bar scene or even simply grabbing dinner with friends.

Honestly, I didn't even want to. But I couldn't admit that to myself. Otherwise, I was letting another piece of me go. You see, I was FUN before this entire mom shit show. Now I just sit here in my dirty nursing bra and diaper while my baby sucks the life out of me all day long. Everyone else moving forward, living their exciting, fun, and powerful lives around me.

What I told myself that I would NEVER be was exactly what I was becoming.

I was turning into the boring, stay-at-home, suburban mom that I ignorantly judged, criticized, and even made fun. That sounds terrible to write out loud, but for years, I had assumptions and internal stereotypes of the SAHM in suburbia.

As I was facing huge changes and cashing in some massive reality checks, I remembered those talks with my friends over endless drinks, exclaiming, "I'll NEVER move to the suburbs!" or "I can't IMAGINE not working!" or "I'll NEVER lose myself in motherhood!" Losing myself in motherhood had me creating a hopeless story inside my mind. The story was filled with a life being consumed by my baby which led me to be the most boring, lost, and insignificant woman I never thought I would be. I didn't know what to do to change this story.

What's really going on, Mom?

As human beings, a certain life is a safe life. It's comforting. We are confident in our lives when there is certainty. Before becoming a mother, you were probably certain what career path you were taking, what your passions were, your interests, and you were confident in the skin you were in.

Even though people will say you chose this new life, when you are thrown into the wolves with this new role as Mom, all that certainty gets tossed out the window. Everything that occupied your time, and your life, is officially on HOLD indefinitely. You are starting over in a big way, and that's the most uncertain and vulnerable place to be in.

There's no time or energy to even think about your passions, interests, strengths, and dreams when you're in survival mode. Deep in the trenches of no sleep and keeping a human being alive that's 100 percent dependent on you, any free time you do have, you can't imagine catching up on sleep as the anxiety grows from all that's on hold and piling up.

There's also this human need to feel SIGNIFICANT. We want to be unique and be recognized for it. We want validation that we are special. As a new mom, even though I had created a human being inside of my body, and was now keeping her alive, I still felt insignificant in the world. How much more significant is human creation?! I had never felt so insecure, imbalanced, confused, lost, and disconnected from who I thought I was.

The problem is, we as moms are defining significance based on other people's terms. The result is you creating expectations and stories about yourself that aren't even close to the reality of your new life. You become overwhelmed, angry, and like me, even depressed. In turn, you run from your new life, your new role, and finding your new significance as a mom.

I am right there with you, sister

I thought I had life all figured out, just like you. I was damn confident with it too. When it came to this mom gig, the books I read, the classes I took, and the advice I received made everything seem pretty doable. At least as far as raising a baby went.

However, there wasn't a class, book, or even a friend who gave me any advice on how challenging this new role would be for me to adjust to. I didn't hear anyone talk about having an "identity crisis" and why a mom would even have one. I felt selfish for even taking time to be sad about missing the city, the fun person I "once was," the successful career I created, and for being an interesting person before shit hit the fan.

I thought something was missing, and for some reason, this baby and being a mom wasn't fueling me like other moms I'd talk to. This shame was shutting me up, probably like you. The one thing that slaps shame in the face is finding the strength to find another human and talk about what you're going through. Bonus if it's someone that can be compassionate, or empathetic, without judgment. Unfortunately, I didn't find anyone to talk to, and today I find myself saying,

Someone failed to mention ...

1. I would have so much insecurity of who I was as a mother and a woman.

2. I would long for the person I was before I had children.

3. I would feel so boring and one-dimensional.

4. I would have no idea how to bring back the things that made me "interesting."

5. Where I lived, my career, or my social life does not define me.

6. The more I ran from my new life, the harder it would be to create one I would love more than the one I left.

7. I'm not selfish if I want to find things to enjoy outside of motherhood.

Let's flip the script

As a new mom, you may find the focus is on everything but yourself. Other than a meal train or your doctor telling you your third-degree tear is healing nicely, no one else is looking out for you either. It's easy to be sucked into a new reality where you feel anything but control of your life.

The beauty is, my friend, you are in 100 percent in charge of your happiness, confidence, dreams, passions, and choices in life. It just takes time and work to get there. Someone else's opinion, harsh words, Instagram post, feelings, and reactions do not control your life. Really? Really. That may sound impossible, but at the same time, it's probably one of the most liberating ways of living as a mom. What's even better is it's true.

You also control and choose the meaning behind everything that comes your way. If you don't believe that statement, just think of a situation where two people are given the same news that they have terminal cancer. Why do you think one person goes into a deep depression, carries anger, continues to eat unhealthy foods, avoids interacting with people, and thinks God is against her?

The other is yes, still scared shitless, and may have a period where she is angry, depressed, and lost. She acknowledges and honors her feelings. But she then chooses how to use these feelings to live the best life possible. She desires control of her destiny. She exercises more, researches cancer fighting foods, hires a health coach to help her, travels the world, surrounds herself with uplifting people, and welcomes all that life can bring her. Same news, different meanings, and therefore, different lives. Which one would you want to live? It's time to flip the script.

Do you want a life where:

- You are in control of finding your passions?
- You choose the meaning behind everything that comes your way?
- You are confident in your purpose of being on this earth?
- You know you are important?
- You choose who is in your life and who makes you feel important?
- You are certain you are where you should be in life?
- You are proud to tell the world you're a mother, without the word "and" after it?

(I hope your answers to all the above is a big HELL YES!)

Let's break the patterns (and expectations!) that are holding you back

Instead of yearning for the life we had, continuing to be sad about it, even resentful, we should be *connecting* to our new life. Whether you like it or not, there has been a massive change in your life where your past may not completely align with where you are now. I was constantly looking back at what I had been doing for the past twenty years. Where instead I should have been sitting in the present, connecting to my inner compass with what I really wanted out of life and what made me unique.

It wasn't because I could drink eight vodka tonics and dance on tables. It wasn't because I performed well at my job and was an asset to my company. It wasn't because I lived in an apartment in the city versus a house in the suburbs. Yes, all were important to me, but they don't tell the actual story of the woman I am, the mom I am. Plus, I find it pretty boring when all people talk about is their jobs, kids, or meal planning. Wouldn't you rather talk about interests, passions, dreams, goals, and what makes life interesting for you? Don't know what those are or where to even start? Stay tuned.

The expectations we put on ourselves, many times based on other people or society in general, are also preventing us from living the amazing life we are meant to live. When we hold unrealistic expectations inside of us, those voices inside our head eventually become our reality. We then believe them. Then we drift further from the destination we are truly meant to land on. Expectations limit us. Most times they cause disappointment.

Our motivation can be put out like a match. I'm trying damn hard to live life under my own realistic expectations. At times, I don't even have any, and let me tell you, it has allowed me to follow my heart more.

The chaos of comparison also affects what we expect of ourselves as moms. Nowadays it's conveniently at our fingertips as we mindlessly scroll through mommy influencers, "badass boss moms," moms who got their "bodies back," or simply through your friends' accounts obsessively wondering what everyone else is doing. Spending that much time and energy on other people's lives that have nothing to do with yours. Wasted time. Wasted energy. Wasted focus.

Before you scroll through social media in a healthy way, you first need to clear out the chaos and commit to finding out what makes YOU happy. What you want in life. Remove the negative story that you're creating in your head and write your own damn story. Comparison puts the energy, work, and responsibility on the wrong person. Remember what I told you: you are 100 percent responsible for your happiness.

I continue to work on removing the word "never" from my vocabulary. This word, "never," created some pretty high expectations and plans that I had in my brain even before I met my husband. Brooklyn just happened to be the reality that put a wrench in all of those "nevers," but it can happen in so many other ways in a mom's life. "Never" can create that unrealistic perfection and judgment where most of the time you will find yourself eating your words or having unnecessary anxiety.

I was the mom proclaiming, "I'll NEVER feed my daughter formula!" Insert foot in mouth. Then there was, "I'll NEVER put toxic chemicals on my baby!" My other foot goes in. I continued with, "Oh my daughter will NEVER get ear tubes; there has to be an essential oil for that!" Twenty-three ear infections and two failed hearing tests later, she was getting ear tubes. There are more. I don't have enough feet to cover them all.

There were so many books that I read to prepare me to be a mother. By mother I mean in the sense of how to take care of my baby. Not myself as this entirely new person. I only wish the books I read included advice and tips such as:

- "You don't have to be a superhero saving the world, life of the party, or a CEO to be important on this earth."

- "Allow yourself to commit to healing first so you can become stronger to figure out your new role in this new life of yours."

- "Be patient as this new you will take time to find."

- "Leaving or taking a break from something at the right time doesn't mean you're a failure. It will make you stronger."

- "Live multi-passionately and explore things that you never thought you'd be interested in. Take chances, live with some risk, and you may possibly discover a whole new you."

- "Your life has completely changed. It's inevitable that you have become an entirely new person; don't run from her. Don't be ashamed. When you accept this new life and new role, only then will you feel confidence in your life."

The power of YET

Whenever Brooklyn's kindergarten classmates said they couldn't do something, their teacher told them to add the word "yet" at the end of their sentence. I think this is a powerful exercise for adults and also lessens the anxiety to feel we need to do all and be all in order to feel significant. It also takes away the permanence of something. To know your situation isn't forever or the end-all-be-all can release the pressure. So next time you say,

- "I don't want to go back to work ..."
- "I don't know what I want out life ..."
- "I don't have time to write my book ..."
- "I don't want to work out ..."
- "I'm not ready for that art class ..."
- "It's not time to make new mom friends ..."

I want you to add the word "yet" to all of them. The desire is in you, otherwise you wouldn't even be thinking of these things. Lessen the anxiety and give yourself time, have some patience, and do it when it feels right. And if you don't do it, that's OK too.

Guided by girlfriends

Get together with some good gal pals and either write on note cards or talk about one another's strengths and what you admire about each other. It's OK if you need to hear it from others in order to fully believe how amazing you are and why you're important. There may be something that you've tucked away and forgotten where you need that reminder!

Writing it down is my favorite way to do this so you can save the cards and pull them out when you're having a hard day. These reminders can reconnect you to why you're unique and all the gifts you give to the world.

Be open to new possibilities

Learning how to be open to the possibilities of life, new experiences, new friends, passions, and creative outlets can make you realize your identity is far beyond your career, where you live, how you dress, how much you party, how often you travel, what you do for fun, or the mother you are.

BIG NEWS: There's an actual person inside of you with other things that fuel your soul and personality.

There are some amazing qualities about you that have may be hiding behind your career, the lifestyle you had, or the person you believe you should be. And like I said above, you are powerful and have 100 percent responsibility to figure out this new you.

I hope you accept this challenge.

And at the end of the day

I've learned through the years that it's OK to switch gears for a bit. To open your mind to other creative outlets that work better for you in this season of life. This is the best way to take down the barriers, ease the pressure, and finally create a connection to the woman you truly are beyond the role of "mom." What's even better is realizing that nothing is permanent. You always have the option to pause, connect with how you're feeling, acknowledge what's working and what's not, and try another path.

Maybe it's not the time to be working full-time; maybe it is. Only you can answer that. Perhaps you can't go to Mexico for a week with other couples, but someday you'll be able to or may not even want to. The freedom that you took for granted may be hard to let go of during this time, but someday you'll be able to have it again, and you'll appreciate it more. Remember, the power of "yet" is always there for you to use.

I wish

I wish someone had told me that I was a unique woman, aside from my career, and that I could still feel important by connecting with my own strengths.

I wish that I wasn't so judgmental and close-minded to geography, and that I could make any place happy and fulfilling with the family and friends surrounding me.

I wish that I could have seen that my humor and fun spirit were still in my heart and soul; they were just being muffled by the urgencies of motherhood that made me too fucking exhausted to find them.

I wish I knew how important it was for me to dig deep for other passions and interests that hadn't been unleashed yet, and how to do this.

I wish I had the books, podcasts, groups, friends, and community I have today to share all the ways they figured out their purpose beyond motherhood.

I wish a friend had told me how it was OK to find what made ME happy versus always on call for my baby's needs. To know how to work through the mommy guilt so I can spend time connecting to who I am beyond the "exhausted mom" label.

Your truths

Motherhood is a lot of work; it's the toughest adjustment you'll ever encounter. Your role has changed, rules are different, and massive shifts have occurred. You are a woman beyond your career, how busy you are, what you post on Instagram, and what your kids are doing.

You are also a woman beyond motherhood and deserve to find things that bring you joy and significance. You are beyond any label and should refuse to be boxed in as the "cool mom," the "crunchy mom," the "hot mess mom," the "positive parenting mom," "the fitness mom," the "organic mom," the "stay at home mom," or the "working mom."

You are a unique woman who has the choice and power to adapt to your ever-changing world and stay connected and true to your unique self.

It is time to go out and find her.

CHAPTER 3

Having a Baby Didn't Complete Us

You haven't even unpacked from the honeymoon. A text pops up from your mother-in-law: "So when are you having a baby?!" I mean can I enjoy sex without getting pregnant for a hot second?!

Over a latte, your best friend tells you how a baby made her marriage even "stronger." As she holds her sleeping baby, she tells you how it has "bonded" her and her husband even more with this magical being they ACTUALLY created together. Are we in a Hallmark movie or something?!

The words "complete," "fulfill," and "bliss" get thrown out so casually one can easily drink the Kool-Aid and believe this is the way healthy family creation goes. I've taken some sips of the Kool-Aid as well my friend. I would watch movies, *Days of Our Lives,* read books, along with listening to women telling me about how motherhood has changed their relationship for the better. I've witnessed women admit that amidst their relationship challenges, they believed that having a baby will be the solution. Life would either be:

A. Complete

B. Fulfilled or

C. Full of "bliss" as this baby would appear
to solve all the world's problems.

Nine years into this motherhood gig, I couldn't disagree more. Even though,

> *I'm still married*
> *I still love my husband*
> *I'm grateful we had a baby*

I'm here to say the correct answer for me is:

D. *None of the above*

Let's start with the obvious

There are wrenches thrown into a relationship after having a baby. They are common, bound to happen, and have thousands of mommy memes to prove them. These wrenches affect the bedroom aspect of our relationship and seem to be the only things we read about or focus on. Let's go through this burnt-out list together:

You're exhausted.

Your boobs have been kidnapped by an infant.

Your vagina looks like a fruit roll up and burns.

Your nipples are bleeding.

You're wearing a diaper.

The noise of your breast pump isn't music for foreplay.

Your boobs leak all over your partner. Oh, and pardon that nursing pad that just fell on your face.

You're wearing a tan nursing bra instead of a lacy push-up bra.

Emotions and moods are ever-changing.

For fuck's sake, you just don't feel like having sex.

I remember going to my "joke-of-a-six-week appointment" with Brooklyn. I sat in the cold room with my exam gown already ripped, trying to hide my bra and underwear. Brooklyn screamed in her car seat the entire time. In the end, based on the progress of my healing vagina and uterus, my OBGYN exclaimed, "You're perfectly fine to have sex!" Oh goodie! Now I can go off to relieve my husband's boner incessantly poking my back in the morning as if to say, "Hey there, in case you don't remember, here I am!"

If your partner's standards are anything like mine, they don't care what bra you're wearing or what bodily fluid leaks on them. Me, not so much. I needed a lot more healing, both physically AND mentally. I wasn't there at six weeks. And you know what? God created hands for a reason, two for a bonus.

Doctor, you seem to have missed something

Looking back, what's insane to me is NO ONE checked my emotional state as a new mom. I wasn't prepared for how I would possibly feel about my husband when I walked into our home with our new baby. Fuck, I wasn't prepared for how I was going to feel about MYSELF.

You know the generic, overly Xeroxed postpartum feelings checklist you get at your OBGYN visit? Or if not there, maybe your pediatrician gives you one while your baby is screaming or having an up-the-back blowout? How is your pediatrician going to be able to help you, and what will they do if you are honest?

Along with that checklist, I want you to bring this bad boy below to your appointment. Let's see what your doctor says about *these* feelings.

Grab a pencil and answer the below with one of the following: Somewhat Agree/Agree/Somewhat Disagree/or Disagree. Feel free to add the word "Strongly" to any of your answers:

1. I have zero desire to have sex.

2. I feel like I'm doing everything for the baby while my spouse/partner does whatever he/she wants.

3. I am too exhausted to have sex.

4. I feel so gross that I don't even want to sleep with MYSELF.

5. I have anger toward my spouse/partner.

6. I have resentment toward my spouse/partner.

7. I want my boobs left alone; they're attacked enough by the baby.

8. Not even a good old-fashioned college buzz will get me to have sex.

9. I'm thinking about fifty other things and sex ain't one of them.

10. My spouse/partner pretends nothing has changed while for me, EVERYTHING has changed.

There is so much emphasis on the physical part of your healing. What about what's going on inside of that beautiful mind of yours? What will connect you with your partner to even *want* to have sex. No one, including yourself, is even addressing how important all these emotions are and how they affect your relationship.

The first baby step you need to take is to *acknowledge* all the emotions you are feeling. Use the checklist I have above and also add to it with honesty and bravery. Awareness of what is going on in your head is the #1 step toward healing. Before you even begin talking about it all, start small and simple by acknowledging what is going on inside of you. This brave decision will allow you to move forward versus being stuck in the same spot feeling as if there's nothing you can do. My mom has drilled this into my head and continues to: *nothing changes if nothing changes.*

The calm before the shit show

I walked in through my door for the first time with Brooklyn. I gently rested her car seat down, looked around, and wondered what Twilight Zone episode I had just walked into. Even though everything around me still looked familiar, I had this overwhelming feeling of starting over. I glanced over at my husband and he, too, physically looked the same but there was now this unfamiliar feeling coming over me. I didn't even think about all the changes that happened two days prior, nor knew of the changes that were about to hit me in the face now that we were home. I wasn't prepared for how much this baby, and all the things that happened to my body, and eventually my mind, were going to affect the marriage I thought was the strongest part in all of this.

My husband had taken the week off work to help and spend time with us. It was so nice not only to have the company, but to also have someone who had been there and done that with my stepchildren. Changing her diaper for the first time had me asking, "Why is her poop bright orange and looks like there are sesame seeds in it?" When he explained, I responded with, "How the fuck do you know all this?" He knew positions, techniques, tips, how to burp her the best way, and most importantly, it was just nice to have time together.

There was this aura in our home where it seemed like it was just the two of us. Brooklyn was so peaceful that first week, she barely made a peep. My party-pooper husband told me that Brooklyn would eventually "find her voice." Even though he seemed to know so much, I didn't believe him and enjoyed the "bliss."

Why does HE get to have all the fun?

The familiar dreaded Sunday night feeling came upon me. It was a feeling I experienced throughout school and in my Corporate America life. I didn't think it would come back as a mom. Anxiousness came over me as Sunday evening approached. I stared at the clock, counting down the hours before he would be going to bed. Which meant my night was just beginning.

The next morning arrived. I heard him turn on the shower and his waterproof radio blasting his AM sports radio station. These two sounds gave me a bolt of anxiety every Monday through Friday as I knew their meaning and what was next.

Grabbing his phone off the counter, and then his car key, he'd come over to me and Brooklyn on the big brown couch that we lived on and said his goodbyes. When the door shut and the deadbolt clicked, it was if my prison cell was being locked. He had to go back to work, so what right did I have to be sad, anxious, or lonely? Or even worse, resentful.

But these feelings were real, and could anyone blame me?

After all, HE was returning to work.

HE was picking up Starbucks for his hour-long commute BY HIMSELF with peace, quiet, and a good audio book.

HE was interacting with grown-ups.

HE didn't stare at a baby for hours with endless reruns of "Golden Girls."

I was jealous of all that he returned to with such ease. What could I say though? He had to return to his reality, and on top of it, I wasn't contributing to our bank account anymore. I felt like this was out of my control. I kept it inside as I imagined his obvious response would be, *"I understand but I have to go to work. What do you want me to do?"* And I would have no answer. So, what was the point?

Good night, sleep tight, and fuck you

The nights were becoming rough. Brooklyn's "voice" that my husband warned me about had finally come alive. It continued throughout the night where she was up every hour to eat or simply scream. On top of it, I was in breastfeeding HELL as I was trying to figure out why she would latch, then unlatch, seem to be done eating, and then scream five minutes later where the cycle just kept continuing with no end in sight.

It would be 3:30 a.m. and I would hear my mother's words, "There may be a time when you will have to put her down, walk away, and take a breath." I'd put her on the guest bed, pace while she screamed, thinking of how desperate I was for help. But with what? You've probably said the same things I did in my head,

"They have to get sleep, so they're rested for work the next day."

Or if you're breastfeeding like I was,

"Well, it's not like they can get up and help with the feedings … so …"

We keep it inside. We don't make it a big deal. We show up
and shut up.

The resentment continued when he arrived home from work in the afternoon, walking in seemingly refreshed and "ready to go!" with our daughter. On my side, I had felt like two days had slowly passed and I was hopefully being rescued. I was angry that he was so happy to see her, because at the same time I was so quick to hand her off and escape.

I was anything but the woman
he fell in love with

There was shame in how I was feeling toward being a mother. Fear of sharing those feelings with him. Would he think I was a total selfish bitch or God forbid not a good mother? He married me because I was independent,

35

strong, loving, and capable of conquering the world, right? During this time as a new mom, I was anything but these things.

More like scared, insecure, angry, regretful, bored, frustrated, exhausted, and lonely. Thoughts that streamed through my head were of my past self. Scolding my present self:

> *Get a grip.*
> *Get your shit together.*
> *Figure it out.*
> What would my husband think if he found out?
> *She's so pitiful.*
> *My ex-wife didn't act this way;*
> *she handled TWO kids better than this.*
> *This isn't the woman I married.*
> *She's so annoying.*
> *God when will she just get over it and shut up?*
> *Why doesn't she just see someone and*
> *stop bothering me all the time?*

What is the deal here?

There are so many emotions going on within the first couple of weeks of being a new mom. All you want is someone to be supportive, helpful, understanding, and patient, right? I had to dig deep, I mean really DEEP, to figure out what was truly going on and why I had so much resentment, and even anger, toward my husband. You know what the root of all of it was?

ME.

I was jealous that he was going back to work
and his life without a baby.

I was resentful because my boobs were the only source
of food and Brooklyn wouldn't take a bottle.

I was angry that he was sleeping while I was up all night with her because she ate non-stop.

I was worried because I wasn't enjoying the newborn stage when he seemed to love it.

I was so fucking bored all day and resented that he interacted with grown-ups.

I hated the fact that he could walk out that door and do whatever he wanted.

I have more but as you see, all these feelings have the word "I" in them. It took a long time and work to acknowledge that my feelings had everything to do with me. So, what about you?

Write down all the feelings you're having right now. Grab a big ol' notebook and pen and simply write. If there are any feelings that have to do with what your partner or spouse is doing that truly hurts you, there are some tools at the end of this chapter to help you. For now, take a baby step and simply get the feelings OUT of you.

Why does it all fall on me?

There is a belief that as women we are traditionally raised to be the leaders in our home once we become a mother. We are the rock, the foundation, and the strength as we create and cultivate our family and home. Aside from growing our baby inside of us, and birthing it, we buy the clothes, the furniture, the bottles, the non-toxic bath products, the toys, the books, the bows, the bibs, the latest gadgets, the formula, and the food until they are grown adults living out of our home. We do the research on the latest trends, milestones, foods, activities, toys, and anything else our baby should be doing. We download twenty-five apps with all the things we and our baby are supposed to be doing and check the apps daily to make sure we are "on track." Then we are eventually looking at daycare centers, pre-schools, researching public versus private, up until they head to college.

There are the systems and rituals we feel we need to create and enforce. We pack the pool bag with all the essentials to include the pain-in-the-ass nontoxic pasty sunscreen that takes twenty minutes to put on. The diaper bag has an exact system for items that MUST be in that bag and where they are located. We don't even think about buying non-organic strawberries. If the baby doesn't have this exact positioning in her crib, is in a sleep sac, with the sound machine on level four, and blackout shades drawn, she won't nap. Oh, and she must go down at exactly 10:25 a.m. for her nap or you'll miss the window. I need to do an A, B, C, D, E, F rituals before her bedtime—and in that order—so ... oh I'll just do it. If you put on soft music, candles, and get some coconut oil, she loves a good massage, and it helps her fall asleep. One more thing, while you're at Target, before you buy anything, send me a photo so I can make sure it's the right one. I'll be back in an hour, are you *sure* you got this?

A mom friend recently told me,

"Getting my husband to understand that 'invisible task list'—you know—all the shit that gets done without him even knowing ... Dr appointments, meal prepping, social calendars, present buying, gosh even kids clothes shopping (who knew managing my son's wardrobe was so stressful?!) and making sure he has enough weather-appropriate clothes for a full range of events/outings. Speaking of which, he just outgrew all his shoes, so I need to go get him new ones today. It's mostly my fault because I just naturally take ownership of these tasks. I wish hubs noticed it more, so that's definitely a struggle for me."

Why do we carry all the duties, lists, research, scheduling, activities, school selection, clothes shopping, buying birthday presents, meal planning, making dinner, cleaning, laundry, emotional support, and so much more on our shoulders?

For me, it's partly due to my perfectionist Type A personality, along with my fear of losing control. And looking like an asshole that can't handle her shit. I defined my success in motherhood with how much I could put on my plate without having a nervous breakdown in front of people. Even if I had a nervous breakdown, I wouldn't show it nor tell anyone about it. If my husband offered to help, I'd immediately shut it down as if he had ZERO clue what raising a child was like. He would attempt to help without asking, ya know, to be a supportive husband and all, and I would stop him, correct him, and eventually just do it myself.

I would have to be physically AWAY from him and Brooklyn for him to be the father he wanted to be. When I was physically away, which wasn't often, I would be checking in and thinking of all the things he was doing and how they weren't how I would do it.

When this continues, they eventually stop offering and asking. They just look at you as if you're going to handle it. Because the reality is, you will.

Break free from the land of Mommy Martyrdom

I've read enough personal development books and taken dozens of courses to confidently share this powerful news:

We are in control of our reality,
the meaning behind everything that comes our way,
our emotions behind it all,
and most importantly, our actions to create the life we love.

It's a hard pill to swallow, and a scary responsibility, when you feel alone, exhausted and that everything is working against you. What doesn't help is we are so disconnected from our needs, feelings, and what we want because we are overly consumed with keeping a human being alive. There is a lot of work and soul-searching required to change your story from a very negative mindset to one that will create a better life and partnership.

Below are some typical feelings a new mom (or even a seasoned mom!) can have toward their partner. It's time to flip that script and change the negative stories you've created to ones that may get you closer to what you truly need. I encourage you to add to this and really dive into what could be a better story for you and your partner. By no means am I asking you to deny your feelings—NO WAY. Your feelings are real, but let's work to see how your life can change when you realize you have the power to change the story.

Your story may be ...	Change the story to ...
I feel like I'm always the one getting screwed over	I feel like I'm doing a lot and not being appreciated; I need to talk about this with my partner.
He/she doesn't do it the way I want to do it	I have less anxiety when it's done my way, plus I've done so much research that he/she didn't even read. However, I need to be open to learning more and maybe he/she has another good way to do this. I also need to remember that all my baby needs is love and safety and my spouse/partner will give that. I trust my spouse/partner.
It's easier for me to just do it myself	It's hard for me to ask for help, and it takes time and energy to explain it. I need to take a breath and realize the first time I teach him/her may be hard, but it will only make things easier when I allow for help. I don't need to save the world in order to be a good mother.

Why does he/she get to go wherever he/she wants, and I have to stay here?	I do not have to stay in this house. I have a choice. Even if I have to take the baby, I have the power to leave and do something I enjoy. It may not be easy, and I may not be alone, but I have that choice. Eventually it will get easier, and I can give her time with her dad/mom. I don't need to feel guilty for doing something that makes me happy and a better mother in return.
Don't I deserve some time to myself?	This time is challenging, and my baby does rely on me for a lot. Perhaps instead of one large block of time, I can take small amounts of time throughout the day for myself? While the baby sleeps, the dishes can wait, and I can enjoy reading a book. I can bring the monitor out to the patio, get some sunshine, and listen to music. When my partner gets home, I can go on a twenty-minute walk and call my best friend.
He/she should just know how I feel. Can't he/she see I need help? I mean, are they blind?! Or just an asshole?	I need to stop complaining and start communicating how I feel and what I need. It isn't getting me any results. Only I know what I need.
Why am I the one doing all the research on (insert baby item here)?	Perhaps he/she assumes I enjoy doing this, and they don't want to take that away from me? Maybe they're afraid they'll overstep or appear to take over? I can ask him/her to help me research (insert baby item here). I'm excited to see what he/she finds!

I feel like my life has turned upside down while his/hers is the same!	Things have changed a lot for me. However, I haven't asked him/her how it's changed for them? Maybe they are just as overwhelmed and having a hard time too?
How does he/she think I'm sexy in any way with this body I now have?	My body is different, and it's going to take time to heal. It may never get "back" to where it was, but it is pretty powerful, and I need to take care of it. I need to tell him/her that I need time and to hear some nice things about why they find me attractive that have NOTHING to do with my boobs or ass.

The bottom line is: YOUR STORY WILL BECOME YOUR REALITY. Whether you decide to live in a negative story or the one of growth and change, that's up to you.

In a nutshell ...

When you have a baby, it's inevitable that there will be a shift in the marriage. Newborns overwhelm us. Toddlers exhaust us. Kids consume us. Not only do they consume our time, but our mental wellness tank as well. Where do we then find the time, energy and stability to cultivate our relationship? The truth is, I had zero desire or energy and nothing left to give. I simply trusted he wouldn't leave me, so I went through the motions, believing there would be an end someday. Hopefully we still liked one another when the dust settled.

Change is hard for me. Going through the motions and seeing the days and weeks just fly by into the months and years seemed so much easier. Being numb is more comforting than ripping the Band-Aid and feeling the open rawness. You trust the numbness more than what may happen when you rip that Band-Aid off.

The truth scares me. I'm afraid to ask and actually hear the words confirming my insecurities. I would have rather lived in ignorance than hear his response and take action to change.

Being vulnerable is terrifying. It's also the bravest place you'll be as a mother. I thought it was easier to play the perfection game than to risk being found out that I wasn't "good enough." The irony is perfection will eventually suffocate you, as it did me. Small changes, risks, mistakes, ripping off a Band-Aid, and moving toward something new is the ONLY way to grow. My goal changed to finding the mom I am meant to be, to be proud of my new role, and to find happiness. I then was ready to be a healthy, supportive, and loving partner in my marriage. I was ready to be a team player in this game we call parenthood.

CHAPTER 4

What Do You Do All Day?

"You'll never have to worry about working ever again," my husband proclaimed. Even before we were engaged. Immediately I became defensive and protective, getting ready for battle as if I was being threatened in some way. I hadn't even moved in nor had any remote desire to get pregnant soon and he was about to hold me hostage in a "Leave it to Beaver" episode.

Feelings of dependency took over, which suffocated and terrified me. I felt my value and worth was completely disregarded, which angered me. He didn't seem to consider how hard it would be for me to leave something I worked so hard for. Which made me want to shove my middle finger in his face. Even with all those feelings that took over, (and I transformed into The Hulk for a moment) I now know he wasn't there to control me or hold me back from my dreams. No one has that power.

In the face of reality

From the day I found out I was pregnant, I realized I couldn't go back to my career. Not only because of the four hours of daily commuting and constant travel. Most importantly it wasn't a mom-friendly environment to the kind of mom I wanted to be. This was 2013, and the company I worked for didn't have work-from-home opportunities or even flexible work schedules for moms. I couldn't even access my email remotely when I was traveling on business. We didn't even have cell phones.

The last thing I wanted to do was to start job searching during my maternity leave. Starting over just sounded so exhausting and painful. As a new mom, I was already in enough of that. My vagina was on fire, I barely had the energy to wash my armpits with a baby wipe, I was lucky to have two hours of sleep, and my boobs were on duty 24-7. But what else was I going to do? I refused to be the SAHM I promised I'd never be. In the meantime, another big foot was prepared to be inserted into my mouth.

Being home to raise Brooklyn wasn't good enough. I created this ridiculous crock of shit and believed it was true. Remember my single friends and I and the ignorant scenarios of what life would be like as a SAHM in the suburbs? My friends and I would then talk over vodka lemonades about all our "I could never" situations:

"I could never leave my career; I've worked too hard for it."
(Valid point.)

"I could never be home all day with my kids." (I get it.)

"I could never 'lose' myself." (I've been there)

"I could never settle for that life—how boring!"
(Yes, it can be boring, but we'll get to that chapter later.)

There were the office water cooler chats with women I worked with or traveled with. Someone would announce they were pregnant, and we'd nosh on cafeteria lasagna, declaring how we would handle motherhood. Our relaxing dinner after sales calls would be interrupted by our friend having to pump. That natural necessity was going to make her come back to cold calamari. And she wasn't drinking on top of it. We would NEVER stop working. We'd hire a nanny. There's no way we'd breastfeed and pump. Our husbands had "better step up!" It was our own picket line defending our worth and not allowing motherhood to destroy it.

The un-real housewives of (insert city)

If you're a *Real Housewives* franchise fan like me, you may have been addicted to the *Real Housewives of Orange County*. If not, still read on. This show consisted of women living in Orange County where a film crew would follow them and their lives. It's far from our reality, but there is one cast member who will always stay in my mind. Ladies, I present to you the judgmental and oh so outspoken Vicki Gunvelson.

Lying on my couch, binge-watching six seasons, had workaholic and "independent" Vicki question every SAHM's day and how they justified their existence, "Well, what does she DO all day? Does she work?!"

I should have realized it was reality TV. Nothing on reality TV, nor any form of media, is going to find an average mom's life exciting, glamorous, or marketable. The middle ground just isn't as exciting.

What are we running from, and WHY?

We live in a society that, keeps women stuck. Creating doubt in our worth and insecurity with what we offer as mothers. We can have pride in movements within our career. Boast about running the NYC Marathon. Cheer as she strengthens her body back from cancer. Yet, birthing a human and raising a human doesn't seem worthy of celebration. Why is motherhood not exciting enough?

Our worth on this earth seems to be tied to how we contribute to society economically. That doesn't change when you become a mother. As a result, we find ourselves endlessly trying to prove our worth and questioning our value as mothers. This is bullshit. Why do we seem to run from the word "Mom" instead of embracing and wearing that badge with pride?

"So, what do you do?"

Nothing is more boring than the "So what do you do?" opening line at a party. It has become the standard "get-to-know-you" question. How do you answer this? Do you find yourself explaining excessively? Proving your days are enriching and exciting? Perhaps you feel being a mom isn't valuable enough where you overcompensate with, "I'm a mom and I also …"

I don't know about you, but lately when I really want to get to know someone, the last thing I want to hear is kid talk or shop talk. I'm OK with a little. I'm not heartless. Can we ask one another about our dreams? Travels? Goals? Let's get to know the REAL person. The real you.

Don't panic. Don't start to create some uncomfortable run-on sentence overexplaining yourself. Let's prep you a bit for your next gathering. This exercise will not only connect you with who you truly are but eventually give you confidence to talk about it. Beyond mom.

Sure, tell them you're a mom. Tell them your career. Don't deny these things. But don't allow it to be your only descriptions or make up shit just to prove you're doing something. Get a pen. Now. No need for paper, I've got you covered below.

Write down five adjectives that describe you:

1.

2.

3.

4.

5.

Now, write out three passions and interests as if you're still or going to be doing them. (Because you will eventually be doing them!)

1.

2.

3.

Keep these exciting answers tucked in your mind for the next time you meet someone. Allow them to get to know the *real* you. Better yet, allow yourself to get to know the real you.

What's a new mom to do?

I sat on that train to work with a harsh reality as I stared at my belly. I was going to be a SAHM. As if it was some degenerative disease. OK, so one thing I knew was that I wasn't returning to the career I built the last fifteen years, but I had no clue what was next.

I became passionate about wellness after hiring a health coach when I was trying to conceive. I began to read these words shouted from the social media mountain tops: "Make money doing what you love!" "Be your own boss!" "Set your own hours!" "Fabulous opportunity for moms!" "Make six-figures!"

Through these nine years of entrepreneurship, I now know that creating and running your own business is ANYTHING but easy, luxurious, or quick. If anything, it's MORE time consuming and connected to your heart. Most won't tell you that you're constantly ON. They seem to leave out that to be "six-figure-successful," it truly isn't a 9–2 p.m., Monday through Friday kind of life. Oh, and you're keeping a human alive who interrupts life constantly, keeps you from sleeping, and mentally exhausts you.

Nobody tells you any of this. That mompreneur on stage may scream how badly she wanted it, so she simply "went for it." Honor your dreams.

Take chances. Start before you're ready. Just "hustle" and you'll make it! But again, nobody is telling you the real way it all happened for them.

Maybe you found the magic potion but in my world, it wasn't working like everyone promised. I found myself constantly frustrated that I wasn't this glamorous and successful health coach I'd see on social media who still finds time to be an amazing mother and make money while she sleeps. I should have known the moment she mentioned that she actually slept that she was full of shit.

Here's my real scenario that works for me. I've chosen hours where as soon as Brooklyn gets off that bus, my computer is shut down. When she's sick, I don't work because my mind is too distracted, and I have huge guilt issues that take an entire chapter in this book. I also allot time in my week to clean my house, cook meals, and do the whole "homemaker gig." For me, I love being at home as much as I am. I have truly desired the time I spend with Brooklyn, but I also needed something special for myself.

Nine years later, I'm just starting to be honest about what I want for this perfect "career" I'm searching for. Honoring the season of motherhood that I am in. What fits in my life. What is already fueling it. Creating my own story that works for me is a lot of work and takes time. Patience.

I'm also paying attention to what fills me up and what ignites the passions inside of me, along with the time I spend with my family. I want to be real, true, and loyal to what makes me happy and fuels the mother and woman I am meant to be. Not what I feel I should be. The truth is, the word "should" has nothing to do what with I want.

Since I don't work in an office outside my home, I won't pretend I can speak for the many mothers who do. Some are my best friends and family. Most seem happy with their careers and the choice to return to them, but there is still the constant questioning if it's enough. Their Mom role doesn't just disappear when they go to work. The moment they walk into their

49

home, they switch hats but still may be detoxing from work-mode. There isn't an easier situation or anything to even begin one-upping.

And if you want proof that comparison is a waste of time here? For every working mom that isn't spending "enough" time with their kids, there is the SAHM mom that is putting their child in front of a TV for "too long." What you don't know is that working mom may have had a big project and pressures that week. But the following week, she took vacation time to spend with her family. The SAHM had just spent three days with two children with the flu where she was on-duty 24/7 and needed that screen time to simply breathe.

My point is, we are all in the same shit storm but different boats with this mom gig. You don't need to exhaust yourself, doubt yourself, or prove something that doesn't deserve the energy.

"YOU ARE MADE FOR MORE!" ... or are you?

There are messages out there that *attempt* to motivate us moms to be the "best" we can be. For some reason, we still walk away feeling like we aren't doing *enough*.

There's that word again. ENOUGH. Why are we constantly told (and believe) we need to do *more*? What if what you're doing is enough? Do you really need to doubt that? As a personal development junkie, I am always open to finding new mentors to connect with, learn, and grow from. It's in our blood to crave growth. There are many motivational speakers, authors, and Instagram influencers telling us we need *more*, deserve *more*, and need to work harder for *more*. They seem to be shouting at us, even scolding us, as if we don't realize how unfulfilled our lives are. I mean, how dare we *only* do what we are currently doing? In my eyes, this "you deserve more" movement is not only bullshit but is giving the same "you are not enough" message that we are trying to get the fuck away from. Taking us further from connecting to what really fuels our hearts. And being damn proud of it.

I will admit, the main problem I had was that I was following the wrong people's stories and advice. Their messages clearly resonate with many, or they wouldn't be as successful as they are.

As a mom whose workday ended once her child hopped off the bus, I needed to take a hard look at whom I was following. Do they have a dramatically different life than I do? Are their goals nowhere near mine? Do they have different core values than me?

I found my "inner filter" to be in tune if the person motivated me or frustrated me. If I had anxiety with their message. If the goals, values, and life that person was living aligned with my life in any way. I stopped reading books by people who had no children, traveled constantly, worked 100-hour weeks, or never saw their family. There's nothing wrong with their lives. They are just dramatically different than mine, so why would I even entertain a lifestyle or goals that simply aren't realistic for me? Why would I have expectations and results that I wouldn't be able to (or want to) achieve?

What's really going on mom?

Human beings, and especially moms, have a deep internal desire to know our significance in the world. We need to *feel* important, valued, and that we are making a difference. We need to be *told* this.

There is disconnect with this need when we become mothers. We question our SIGNIFICANCE in the world, to a point where we become the most insecure we've ever been. Which results in the "one-upping," comparing, justifying, searching, getting in the "I'm so busy!" trap, and proving to others what our purpose on earth is as mothers. Why are we on a never-ending search to find, and prove, our significance?

My past career success was always *measurable*. If you're familiar with goal setting and achievement, having goals that are measurable is essential. When I became a mother, I didn't have any of that. Not even ONE day. It was the exact opposite.

We also have the desire to GROW, which can be lost in motherhood, as we tend to focus on that other human being that's growing. What's beautiful about growth is that its form is unique to everyone based on what's important to them as an individual. Yet another reason not to compare!

Another human desire is to GIVE and CONTRIBUTE to the world. Unfortunately, like I said earlier, society seems to tie our value and worth to financial and economic contribution. Otherwise, your passion is "just a hobby," a waste of time, or doesn't really matter. Says who, and who is making the rules here?!

I will tell you this right now: Your value is not tied to what you deposit into the bank. It's time to change your belief in what your worth *truly* is, what you can give yourself and the world around you, and why you're needed on this earth. Keep reading, and we can figure out how— together.

Someone failed to mention ...

1. I needed to honor my guilt with my decision to leave my career and figure out how to *work with the guilt* versus ignore it or get stuck in it for too long.

2. That quitting something doesn't mean I'm a failure (thank you Marie Forleo). It may simply mean I needed to say goodbye to something that wasn't meant for this season to welcome something that is.

3. My dreams don't need to make me famous to matter (Thank you About Progress).

4. That I should have connected more with what I appreciated in that moment versus always thinking of the past and all that I let go of.

5. Whether I stayed at home, went back to work, or tried to create world peace, people were already judging me. So why not just do what makes me happy?

6. Knowing what I wanted was the hardest part.

7. I have a strong desire to grow, and motherhood made me feel like I wasn't.

8. I didn't need a salary to feel important or that I'm contributing to my family and world around me.

9. My goals for my life can change and evolve. That doesn't make me a flake.

10. I'm not indecisive or a hot mess because I want multiple things in my life. It's beautiful to have many passions and to explore them.

11. That I needed to pay attention to the season of life I was in and what truly worked for me. Just because I couldn't do it at that time, didn't mean I could never do it. (Thank you Michael Hyatt)

12. I'm going to doubt the HELL out of myself and a LOT. I wish I knew those were the best times for me to check in and see if I needed to make any changes, take a new path, or say goodbye to something.

13. That as moms, we push our own dreams way down deep inside because it's in our nature to take care of others first.

14. That if my dream didn't happen right away, that was normal! Dreams can take time, especially when I'm raising a human. I wish I knew how to find patience in an instant gratification world.

15. That I was going to feel guilty no matter what decision I made.

I wish I knew ...

That I had to find and honor the creativity that is inside of me. I lost this when I was focused on my career and then swallowed by motherhood. When I read Elizabeth Gilbert's book, *Big Magic,* I finally connected to what made me uniquely me. Why I'm on this earth, all I can give to others, how I learn, grow, and eventually find the confidence in the woman I truly am.

It was a lot of work to uncover my creative friends that were patiently waiting inside of me, but I eventually listened to them. There were things in my life that I had to turn the volume down on in order to hear the special gifts inside of me. I challenge you to not only read *Big Magic* but then to tap into your creative soul to find the real you.

CHAPTER 5

How to Politely Tell Someone to Shut the F Up

From the moment I announced I was pregnant, information hit me from every angle. You know when you simply look at an Instagram ad and suddenly that sweater you thought was pretty is now on your social media platforms. Your Alexa then says in a gentle, robotic whisper, *"Michelle, I found a sweater I thought you'd love."*

That's what happens when you tell just one person you're pregnant. Word travels fast, and then the crowd of fans grows every single day. Sometimes you don't even have to tell someone, you may be like me where the world may simply notice you deny your usual mojito and gasp, "YOU'RE PREGNANT!"

Next thing you know ...

Baby books are donated, advice is given without being asked, ads appear on your social media feed, you'll reach out to "Dr. Google" (along with your own doctor), take a class or two, attend a baby expo (or three), join some mommy Facebook groups, follow various Instagram accounts, and your brain will start filling up with all the "what's best" for baby. These are just half of the resources that will be pounding on your door, and you haven't even touched the second trimester. Questions will flood your conversations such as,

"How are you feeling? Are you eating enough? I don't think you should be exercising like that anymore. You're still traveling for work? Does your diet have enough iron in it? What did your doctor say? She didn't talk about X, Y, or Z with you yet? What kind of a doctor are you seeing? I know someone; let me make a call. Why aren't you _____? Why are you _____? When are you going to _____? How are you going to _____?!"

After I peed on the stick, told my husband, and confirmed with my OBGYN I was pregnant, I started the nine-month process of to-dos, don'ts, shoulds, shouldn'ts, musts, and nevers. My OBGYN, on the other hand, was a wham-bam-thank-you-ma'am doctor. Come on in, legs in stirrups, "open wide!" slide it in, brrrr that's cold, shit that hurts, swab and done. Boobs feel good, ovaries feel fine. See you next year. I would return to work in time to eat a sandwich at my desk.

She had the same strategy with my pregnancy. Her version of "What to Expect When You're Expecting" was in the form of another overly Xeroxed sheet of dos and don'ts for whatever stage I was at in my pregnancy.

"Do you have any questions?"
"Nope!"
"OK, we'll see you again in …"

I always felt like I was wasting her time, and she was in a rush. So, I didn't ask much. I felt this pressure to be fast and low maintenance. Heck, I could always try to figure it out on my own with the forty-seven resources I had, and if I couldn't … *then* I'll ask her. Maybe.

There were the classes offered at the hospital I was delivering at. I chose Breastfeeding 101, Baby CPR (AKA me and my husband laughing and taking selfies with our CPR dolls), and a general "What to Expect" class going through each trimester as well as delivery. I added these to the bookshelf of information stacked in my brain. I mean the more information, the better, right?

What's interesting is at the time I was attending these classes, I felt super confident, and that this motherhood gig was going to be a piece of cake. I felt prepared. I had the tools. But after Brooklyn was born, I never felt so lost. It's as if all that I had learned was forgotten or didn't even apply to us.

My baby shower was another interesting load of information. Products and all the must-haves for my baby and me to have the most magical pregnancy, birth, and beyond. I completed my registry down the aisles of Buy Buy Baby with my sister-in-law's, since she had already done the research. We had our girls around the same time, which made my registry a piece of cake. I scanned what she had along with adding some unnecessary outfits and a few shouts outs of "Hon, do you think we need this?"

Who is inventing all this baby stuff anyways? We all know we didn't have a dizzying amount of stuff when we were babies. My mom cloth-diapered me and basically laid me on the bottom of a playpen to fend for myself. As a toddler, my mom simply put an empty laundry basket next to me to play with. I could make an entire photo album of me in a laundry basket or cardboard box. As a child of the 70s, our moms didn't have as much SHIT as we do now.

We didn't have to stare at an item with its twenty-five different versions, stages, colors, and pricing. Talk about analysis paralysis as I stared at the dozens of bottles and nipples, the baby food makers, things that supposedly made a baby stop crying, sound machines, creams, soaps, cribs, bassinets, swaddlers, sleep sacks, and tummy time toys. What the hell was tummy time anyway?

The REAL, Real Housewives

Brooklyn arrived in the world at 6:27 a.m. By 7:30 a.m., I had a lactation nurse in my room, bringing my baby to me for my first dose of mom reality. I wasn't even given time to longingly stare at my baby. She propped me up with pillows, grabbed my boob, smashed it like a burger, and shoved half of it into Brooklyn's mouth. I want to take a moment to thank Kristen Bell for this analogy (and laugh).

She latched as I sat there in a daze and just stared at her. OK, not so bad. So far so good. If we hit any bumps along the way, I assumed I'd figure it out somehow. The nurse popped in often to remind me to feed her, just in case I forgot as I frantically tried to recreate my boob burger. These women obviously were there to help me, but I felt suffocated as they stalked and stared at my boobs while I fed her.

Two weeks later, the shit show began. Not only was she up all night, but she was *screaming* all night. She would latch but then about a minute into it, she would fly off my boob, screaming. Clueless, I would head to my computer with her screaming in my arms and sit with Dr. Google. I'd tell my husband she was cluster feeding based on that night's research. I'd then return to the computer and read another article, then another, and then another. I'd open a book and frantically search as if a bomb was going off, and I was trying to find the code to deactivate it. I was fucking Mommy MacGyver.

All my resources would have twenty different possibilities that only made me feel more lost. I was desperate for answers that worked. Luckily my pediatrician's nurse practitioner was a lactation consultant, and she immediately told me the answer. I was drowning my baby as if my boob was a hose that was turned on full blast in her mouth. Overproduction. Awesome, I was already failing at the mom gig.

Even though she gave me a sigh of relief with some amazing tips, I got back on Dr. Google to make sure there wasn't *anything* else out there that was missed. I was going crazy researching and getting even more confused. Why didn't I just continue with what she told me and trust the advice, along with myself?

Why don't I know what to do? I'm so confused!

Let's cut to the good news first. Most of the time you DO know what to do. That knowledge is in there, but it's just hidden by our huge fears of failure, looking stupid, screwing up our baby, others knowing all this, and too much information being thrown at us.

We'll cut to the "what others think" and smash that right now: You don't have to tell jack shit to anyone. Lighten the load worrying about what others will think by just keeping it within the four walls of your home. The analysis paralysis and confusion we have is due to the overload of contradictory information out there. I've survived the battles to tell this. One website says this, your doctor poo-poos it with, "Oh that's just internet garbage!" Your friend tells you that never worked for her, perhaps with a judgmental tone. A book you read then swears by it. Next time you see your MIL, she tells you, "Oh, that's just a bunch of that hippie dippie crap!" You're then left wondering what the fuck is going on and what to do. No wonder we are so confused and full of anxiety as new parents!

We feel there is this *one* magic solution out there for all babies. We keep searching for it. This is massive pressure and totally unrealistic. The reality is, there could be quite a few solutions that could help you get through something. One day it may not work. Another week it does. One child may respond to it; your second one may not. It's kind of a crap shoot at times. Trusting your mom compass, taking risks, being open to making mistakes, and seeing them as learning opportunities (versus failures) will lighten your mental load and anxiety. Allow yourself to open the doors a bit, connect with what speaks to you, and be confident in the decision you make *at that time* for your unique life.

Information changes constantly, and your baby is different!

I step into a baby-related store, and the new products amaze me. I *guarantee* some of the things I did with Brooklyn may not be the answer anymore. When you receive advice, first make sure the advice is from *at least* this decade. Or even the last couple of years. Even more importantly: even if a piece of advice worked for someone else, YOUR baby is entirely different. Your baby may not react or respond to what worked for your friend, and that's normal. Oh, and another thing: You are an *entirely different mother* than the one who gave you advice. Honoring what you are comfortable with, what aligns with your values, and being brave to make decisions based on all this will create the confident mother inside you.

If plan A doesn't work, there's always a B or even C

Some days breastfeeding sucked. Others a breeze. For our nanny, some days pumping a few bottles for her worked. Other days I was shaking bottles with formula. Some days Brooklyn's amber teething necklace kept her smiling. Other days it was Tylenol and a cold washcloth to chew on. There were time periods I used chlorine-free Seventh Generation diapers, and then when her blowouts were so bad I stocked up on Huggies Ultra.

If Plan A didn't work, knowing a Plan B (or even a C) was out there gave me such relief with my anxiety. The rule is that Plan B or C were to be used with zero judgment. I attempted my best option first, but if that didn't work, the next was just as good. I still use this mentality with raising

Brooklyn. Then I don't have to be stuck trying something that doesn't work and brings me to tears.

The key here is not overwhelming yourself with *too many* things though. Have a few options to go through and know it's OK if you ask for help or advice if those don't work. The support will help you where you don't feel lost doing it all on your own.

Know you will be judged

Let's just cut to the chase. Strangers will judge you; your family will judge you; good friends, casual mom friends, and strangers in a so-called supportive Facebook group will judge you. As humans, we judge. I've judged. I still catch myself judging.

We also judge ourselves. EVERY. SINGLE. DAY.

Keep this in mind: Your truth and your story are not the same as theirs. You don't know their entire story the same way they don't know yours. Keep creating your unique story, and like Brené Brown says, only tell it to people that have earned the right to hear it. It's not their job to approve what you're doing, and it's not your job to approve what they're doing. Aren't we busy enough with our own lives? Remember all this the next time you find yourself judging another fellow mom who's just doing her best to get through another day. Like you.

How do you feel when others give you advice? Honor and trust that feeling.

Unsolicited advice, questions, or feeling like the eyes are always watching create a mountain of anxiety. Each of us handles advice and conversations from friends and family differently. Some may feel grateful for the advice and crave it. The advice you receive may have sincerity and a supportive approach where you appreciate it. You may feel relieved, and the advice worked for you. Trusting your gut is important, but also trusting your gut when someone *else* is giving you advice is just as important. If it warms you, doesn't overwhelm you, you trust them, and feel drawn to it, then honor those feelings!

But if you are overwhelmed, hesitant, or just want that person to shut up, listen and honor these feelings as well. There is nothing wrong with you. It's OK if you are drawn to look deeper into what the intention is behind the actual advice. Most advice comes from someone genuinely wanting to help. They lead with love.

There are also times when someone is sticking their passive-aggressive, know-it-all nose in your business. They lead with self-doubt. It's what I call *internal judgment* within the person and is the motivation for the advice that is so generously given to you. The person tells you "what's best" to make them feel better about their own choices. They don't even realize it. If you're feeling tight, anxious, and immediately defensive when someone opens their mouth or types a comment, pay attention to these feelings so you can disconnect from the advice.

Find your "people"

Consider the source and the feeling you get. Next, I want you to really think about gravitating toward people that give you that "oh so good feeling" when talking motherhood. Find the ones that mean well. Here are the qualifications:

1. People who give you advice when you ask for it.

2. People that acknowledge that every baby is different, but this worked for them, and they simply wanted to share because they love you.

3. People that acknowledge that the advice they give may not work.

4. People that send you a little note saying, "I know it can be hard. I won't pretend that I know what you are going through, or I know what is best. Just know I am here if you need to talk or want help."

5. People that respect your final decision and don't question it.

Creating the "Mom Compass"

Motherhood can be like an episode of *Naked and Afraid*. You're vulnerable in a jungle of judgment, and you need help navigating to survive. How have I survived all these years? Fortunately, it's very simple (yay!), *but* it did take time and a lot of work to get here. There are days I have setbacks, struggle, and must do the work to get back. The good news is you only need one piece of equipment.

I quieted the noise by connecting more to my powerful intuition, my "Mom Compass," versus solely to what everything else was telling me to do. You know, that "mommy gut" that we hear, doubt, and eventually lose connection with. Advice is great, and I took a lot of it to heart, but I also needed to create a filter so I could be clear and confident about what worked best for us.

While I was part of a group at a hospital that spoke to expecting parents, I listened to a life coach talk about this subject where she had the audience write down their top five family values. The trick is to make sure that yours align with your partner's so you both are pretty much on the same page when it comes to raising your family. (Side note: we as mothers don't have to do this parenting thing all on our own. Making sure you welcome and honor your partner's side in all this will create strength and confidence in your choices.) With each challenge and situation that you're faced with, reconnect to these five values that are true to your core. Be proud of them, stand by them, and make sure your decisions align with them. Don't ever apologize for them either. Ever.

Connecting to your "Mom Compass," that mother's intuition, is a lot of work. Intuition is pretty darn powerful, as hokey as you or your partner may initially see it. Maybe thinking about your intuition in the form of instincts instead will be more relatable. We see animals making many decisions solely based on their instincts. That mama duck with her ducklings doesn't have grandma duck following her around quacking. She doesn't have social media access, isn't part of a mommy duck Facebook group, nor can she read. She's not sitting alongside her ducklings overanalyzing what to feed her ducklings. She simply feeds them because her instincts tell her to. She observes her ducklings and responds to them based on what signals they are giving her. Most importantly, she then trusts her decisions.

As human beings with access to a TON of information, the magic equation here is to combine rational thought and facts *with* our intuition. When you're bombarded, your ultimate goals are actively disconnecting from the "noises" of information and finding blank white space that allows you to listen to the voice that is inside of you. It also helps to not look too far into the past or linger with all the "what ifs" of the future that may never happen. Next time your head gets too noisy:

- Pause, taking a breath, and focus on that present moment and what is accurately going on every day.

- Become curious and open-minded to what your intuition is telling you so you can make the most stressful decisions a bit more natural and relaxed.

- Honor your feelings, NO MATTER WHAT. What is speaking to you when it comes to how your baby is sleeping? If you truly want to try the CIO method, try it! If you have this strong feeling a schedule would work better for her and your family; take a chance! If breastfeeding isn't working, and your gut is telling you this is quickly falling down a slippery slope, honor that!

- Mistakes WILL be made, and thank God we make them, as it's the best opportunity for us to connect, listen to our intuition, pivot, and try something new. Eventually YOU will find what works. How amazing will you feel that you've found it on your own versus making every decision based on someone else's experience or opinion?

- Oh, and one very important factor: We also need to trust our partner/spouse's intuition in all of this by communicating and making decisions as a team. Don't assume the mommy instinct is the only player in the game. Navigating the crazy and chaos is much better when you have that teammate on your side.

This is harder than dating

Something really frustrating for both you and your baby is the fact that your baby cannot talk. You cannot understand your baby. I don't know if a baby can understand us, but let's assume they cannot. There is an entirely new communication system that you're both creating to figure all this crap out together. The reality is you may feel alone at times, but at the same time, the beauty in all this is you aren't. You are creating a one of the most important relationships and building a connection. That takes time, patience, and a lot of bumps along with the joy. When you're having a really hard day, these simple tools may help relax and reconnect you together:

1. Take a deep breath in as you count down from five. (Thank you Mel Robbins!)

2. Exhale slowly out your mouth as you count down from five.

3. Look at your baby and say, "We are a team. We are both learning this new world together. We'll get there my friend. Through some tears, we will get through this and so much more."

4. Repeat if necessary. Some days it will be.

NEWS FLASH! In case you didn't know ...

- Setbacks happen.
- There are no guarantees.
- You will doubt yourself, a lot.
- It's OK if you don't have your shit together.
- It's OK if something you're trying takes a long time to get results.
- It's OK if that thing you're trying isn't easy (it's not supposed to be!).
- It's OK if you're so exhausted and want to give up.
- It's OK if there are some tears and screaming into towels behind closed doors.
- It's OK to have a plan B, C, or even D.
- You're going to make mistakes, a lot of them.
- Mistakes are needed to learn and grow.
- You don't have to save the world or do it all on your own.

And at the end of the day ...

Sometimes you don't need advice and solutions. Some days you may just need to vent. Sometimes you just need someone to hug you and tell you that you're doing a great job. The truth here is *you are*. You're figuring out this "dance" with your baby and your partner. You're all getting to know one another and are in this new world together. Be open to the Plan Bs and Cs you'll need to take. View your challenges and mistakes as the best gifts you'll ever receive, be open to learning from them, and create a unique life that is best for you and your baby.

The beauty of taking in the advice is connecting to your core and the feeling you get when you receive it. Does it sound like something that parallels the values and goals you have with your baby? Or do you need to simply say, "Thank you so much" and try something else that sounds better for your unique baby? You cannot control people wanting to help and tell you what they feel will help you, but you can control how you react, how you respond, and the choices you make.

If you're at a loss for words

As we end this chapter, you may be asking, "Michelle, this is all great, but how do I actually *respond* to the people that are telling me what I'm doing wrong and how I should be doing it?!" You can listen to advice, be open to it, and you may even use some of it. But if anyone gives you unsolicited or judgmental advice, there's an easy way out. Here are some simple responses, paired with a fake smile, that you can keep in your back pocket:

"Thank you so much for your advice";
"Oooh, that's so interesting, thank you for sharing!"
(insert sarcasm);
"I didn't know that, thank you!" (I use this one to
quiet the know-it-alls);
"So glad that worked for your child";
Or a simple "Thank you."

The secret here is to keep your response short and sweet to avoid extending the conversation any longer than it needs to be. Respond and react with dignity to create the boundary so the conversation STOPS right there. You don't need to explain a thing. They'll never know if you took their advice or not, and the beauty is it's not their business anyways.

But for the seventy-year-old man that reprimands you at Target for not having socks on your baby during the winter? That man deserves a gentle raise of the middle finger. With a smile, of course.

CHAPTER 6

Maybe I'm Just Wired
for Mom Guilt?

So many tell me not to worry so much, that I shouldn't feel this way, that I deserve to have "me-time," but no matter how much advice I take in, how many social media posts I read, or books that try to guide me away from guilt … I still feel it. When I'm away at work, I feel guilt. If I have a night out with a friend that I haven't seen in months, I cringe as I close the door and hear my daughter crying. It breaks my heart. I don't even bother planning a weekend away with my husband because it's just not worth the feelings I have. Sure, they disappear from time to time, I'm not sitting there wallowing in my tears. But then I talk to my daughter, who is with her grandparents, and even though I know she is having a wonderful time, I hang up feeling guilt for doing what I'm doing and that I should be with her. I feel like I'm neglecting her or missing out on something. Even if I'm gone for an hour. —My blog, *The Honest Mom Blog,* 2016*

My thirty-seven stuffed animals were all lined up in their assigned spots, each had their special place on my daybed and in my life. At just seven years old, I knew they weren't really alive, but my heart would ache if I played or slept with a certain few while neglecting others. It was as if I could feel their feelings being hurt because I didn't pay attention to them. To play with them all at once was a challenge and to sleep with them all an impossibility. Maybe this is why I cry when I watch all the "Toy Story" movies?

At twenty-nine years old, I couldn't even leave my new puppy in his crate while I was at work down the street for eight hours. With my office door closed, I attempted to work, but ended up crying instead. When the anxiety and crying lasted two weeks, my parents came to the city and offered to take my puppy for a week. I said my goodbye to my puppy, and silently realized he wasn't coming back.

My parents alleviated my guilt. Temporarily. Because I couldn't do what I did with a baby.

My guilt, of course, carried into motherhood. I can honestly say I feel guilty about something almost every single day. I'm sure you can guess from my two stories above that one of my main sources of guilt is the amount of time I spend with her. To make every waking, or sleeping, moment as eventful, loving, growing, connecting, and happy as possible. Any moment I was away from her immediately pulsed guilt through my veins.

Expectations have changed, and the pressure is even higher

I don't know about you, but my grandmother didn't spend a third of the amount of time with my mother and her siblings compared to today's standards. When my grandmother was with her children, I know for a fact she wasn't on the ground playing with them and rolling around like a monkey. She wasn't constantly shaking toys in front of her children, carrying them constantly, reading to them all the time, researching all she could buy to make her kids smarter, doing crafts with them, stimulating them, making sure they weren't bored, hovering over them to see what they were doing, and all the countless things I was doing with my daughter. I'd go visit my grandmother with Brooklyn and would stressfully sweat, trying to pull every entertaining trick out of my massive diaper bag, even if she wasn't fussing at all.

"WOULD YA JUST LEAVE HER ALONE FOR A MINUTE?!" screamed my strong-minded Eastern European grandmother from her kitchen table. I ignored her, scrambled in the diaper bag, and thought, "She doesn't realize how hard this is; she doesn't remember or understand." She raised her children in the 50s and didn't get how it was now. Things have changed. Or have they?

I know my mother played with me and my dad read to me, but honestly, I also know my mom was letting us do our own thing a lot. She was raising three kids and had sixty other things to do as well. She didn't have a cleaning lady. There were no Hello Fresh boxes on her doorstep or DoorDash deliveries. My dad worked long hours and traveled from time to time. Do I have any memory of my mother playing with me every moment I was awake? No. Do I have any memory of my mom doing the dishes, vacuuming, cooking, cleaning bathrooms, or wondering why she wasn't playing with me? Nope. I do remember being happy and loved.

Today's standard of time spent with our kids has seen such a drastic change from generations past. I created massive pressure on myself to entertain my daughter. I believed that when Brooklyn was an infant, I needed to be constantly talking to her, shoving black and white books in front of her, placing stimulating and educational toys in reach, singing to her, and staring at her making faces. I never simply let her be, nor let myself be.

When she was a toddler, I felt the need to buy workbooks, flashcards, and apps so I could educate her in between those moments of fun. "They're only little for a short time; soak in every minute!" was playing on repeat inside of my head and heart. It didn't help that I knew she was my "one

70

and done." There was so much anxiety inside of me, along with the guilt if I was falling short. Not doing enough. Not giving enough. What was I overcompensating for?

You know what helped me conquer and work with all my guilty feelings? It wasn't my idea, nor was it due to any research I did, so I can't take the credit. I will take credit for one thing though: I was open to learning and trying new things to change how I felt so I could breathe.

Brooklyn began Montessori school at the age of eighteen months. Two core beliefs of Montessori education are the importance of both independent play and internal motivation. Brooklyn's teachers educated me and helped me understand the importance of her handling her world on her own and how to entertain herself. If I need to make dinner, I can do that where Brooklyn is close enough to me and at the same time she has access to her toys, art supplies, and other things to entertain her while I cook. I set up our family room where our bookshelves were organized with her supplies at her level, and there was a table for her to do what she wanted without me stressing about a mess.

Then I saw how it was all working, as she was becoming confident in her world. She had independence and happiness, and I had a guilt-free time making an awesome dinner for my family. Even today at age nine, she independently goes off for an hour at a time to do her art, make slime, read, build something, or do crafts.

Time away from her was definitely hard for me. It still is at times. Whether it was working a few days a week, going to a yoga class one night, or dinner with an old friend, I created guilt the moment I packed my bag, grabbed my yoga mat or my purse. Sometimes her nanny was with her, at times my mom, and many times my husband. This took time, and some tears from both Brooklyn and me. I vowed to recognize the benefit of Brooklyn being with other people. The different experiences and love she was receiving from the important people in her life all contributed to the girl she was growing into.

I would be self-absorbed to think that I am the only influential person in her life. For example, her nanny, Sally, was a spitfire of a woman with the most beautiful red curly hair and glasses. She was in her 50s, raised a son of her own, and had so much warmth, wisdom, laughter, and energy. She was important for Brooklyn but also for me as we had such wonderful conversations throughout the time she was with us.

Another example is my mom (we call her Gigi). She is such an amazing grandmother with so much to give. Brooklyn and my mom both have this unique connection that I had to allow to grow. Brooklyn deserves that and so does my mom, without me hovering in the background.

My husband needs one-on-one time with his daughter, so he can get to know her without any distractions by, you guessed it, ME. Brooklyn also needs to know that her dad has just as important role in her life as I do. She can't look at me as the only one to rely on, or I will be the only one she will feel she can go to.

Simply the best

Not only is the amount of time you spend with your baby lurking over you, but you also have the pressure to give your child the "best" of everything. Whatever that means to you.

The aisles filled with shelves upon shelves of the BEST baby food.

- Research saying this is the BEST formula.

- Oh, someone told me these are the BEST and SAFEST diapers out there.

- This line of lotion, sunscreens (don't even get me started on sunscreen), soap, essential oils, and diaper cream were rated the BEST by the EWG.

  (BTW, who are these grand masters of determining what's "best" for your baby?)

Then you have the moms in your playgroup discussing these products, ways to sleep train, how to make your child's head shaped the right way, all the benefits of wearing your baby (even though yours screams bloody murder the moment she's wrapped in it), breastfeeding speeches, and ten-minute stories of all the research she's done and how she's read it's the "best."

Shouldn't the experts of your world be in the hands of both you and your partner/spouse? Trying what works for you and being damn proud of finding it—together? Remember, I'm all about being open to advice but it's also important to confidently create that filter so you can connect with your baby and honor what works for you. Even if it isn't known to be the "best." It's the best for YOU, and that's all that matters.

Reality check

Write down your three best memories with your parents as a child. Really reflect on the quality versus quantity when it comes to the creation of these memories. Think about what you learned and how it helped shape who you are. Take some time to think if you truly remember *every single* moment your parents did (or didn't) spend time with you and if it truly impacted the person you are today.

1. _____

2. _____

3. _____

What's really going on mom?

Humans have a strong internal desire for CERTAINTY. I know I do. Unfortunately, in the game of motherhood, the results are many times long-term, and our days are inconsistent and often unknown. In this short-term world with little patience, this can cause the insecurity that we have with raising our children.

I also found myself confused and uncertain about what to do because there always seemed to be this "new way." One day it's this and then the next you see on the Today Show there's a "new way" to do it. One decade says it's safe for your baby to sleep this way, another decade it's not. The blog you're reading tells you about the benefits of being a working mom, and then another blogger tells you it's better for a mom to stay at home.

Not only is all the information confusing, but you also become disconnected from how you want to raise your children and the mother you truly want to be. It can feel like an endless circle where you second-guess and constantly feel you're not measuring up. How do we then tackle these things so we can find some sort of certainty and sanity in this shit show?

Beyond the word "guilt"

Let's first step out from under the blanket term "Mom Guilt" and dive into the more specific and accurate feelings you're having. Check off those that apply for you:

Neglectful	
Anxious	
Incompetent	
Regretful	
Insecure	
Judged	
Worried	
Fear of failing	
Sad	
Angry	
Falling behind or short	
Any others?	

When we generalize and smash all these important feelings we're having into the "Mom Guilt" box, it's difficult to pinpoint where the exact challenges are lying. In turn, it's even more challenging to then figure out how to work with the feelings you're experiencing to come up with solutions to help you. The topic of awareness and acknowledgement of our feelings as moms is so important with this "Mom Guilt" epidemic we are in. It's getting worse and there aren't enough mom memes to save us.

When I did my research, whether it was in-person interviews, books, or articles, my chest tightened just hearing other moms' stories. Top that with my own mom guilt and I'm surprised I didn't have a panic attack. When I did an initial and casual Internet search with the words "Mom Guilt," it was astounding how 95 percent of the articles and blogs I found had to do with working moms. (Yes, we all have mom guilt whether we go back to our careers or not.) I became concerned with each scroll and video I'd watch. Going back to work brought in a wave of women expressing their challenges with this. As a mom who left her career, I don't pretend to know how these women feel, but I can still sympathize and feel for them. Mom Guilt has different meanings to different mothers due to our own unique histories, personalities, children, and stories. Regardless of how we digest all that gets thrown in our face, we are all moms and need to be there for one another.

We are all in this together

Opportunities are presented within every minute of our day to feel guilty about *something*. Every mom out there has these feelings, so you're not alone. You need to find the moms who risk telling you their feelings so you can connect and help one another. Just so you know, we are all feeling many, if not all, of the feelings below ... Are you with us on any of these?

- I feel guilty when I am at work and my baby is with a nanny.

- I feel guilty that I'm the only adult my baby interacts with other than my partner/spouse.

- I feel guilty that I left my job and don't contribute financially anymore.

- I feel guilty that I travel for work.

- I feel guilty for the maternity leave I had and the colleagues that covered for me.

- I feel guilty for the maternity leave I took and now I've decided to stay at home.

- I feel guilty that my maternity leave wasn't enough.

- I feel guilty staying home and all that I put into my career.

- I feel like I spent so much money on college to simply throw my career away.

- I feel guilty that I'm not playing with my baby enough.

- I feel guilty that I don't know what my baby needs when she's crying.

- I feel guilty playing with my baby too much and I'm not getting anything done.

- I feel guilty because the house is a mess, and this baby is strapped to me, eating. Nonstop.

- I feel guilty because I don't want to have sex with my partner/spouse.

- I feel guilty because I am too exhausted to talk to my partner/spouse about things we used to love to talk about.

- I feel guilty that I don't see my friends.

- I feel guilty when I go out with my friends.

- I feel guilty that I don't have any desire to leave the house.

- I feel guilty for snapping at my mom for trying to help me.

- I feel guilty that the baby is so loud at night and everyone's trying to sleep.

- I feel guilty that I have no desire to even shower.

- I feel guilty leaving my baby in her bouncy while I shower.

- I feel guilty that I didn't breastfeed long enough.

- I feel guilty that I am breastfeeding for too long.

- I feel guilty that I chose not to breastfeed.

- Other moms seem to know so much more than I do.

Embrace and work with the Mom Guilt instead of against it

You have the power to choose the meaning behind everything that comes your way. But what if the feelings creep in despite your efforts? Well, I'm here to tell you to first honor those feelings and try to figure out why you're feeling them. Don't brush them under the rug like I did. Don't hide them or deny them like I did. It's OK to spend some time feeling them in order to allow yourself some time to figure out what will get you through them.

There's this "Fuck the Mom Guilt" movement the past few years. I originally thought this campaign was a great way to give the power back to moms to find their happiness. I can see where the intentions come from, to give moms the spirit to not allow Mom Guilt to control them.

The more I've read or listened to this movement though, the more I realize it really doesn't work for me. I'm just not a woman who feels better by simply telling a feeling to "fuck off" and that I don't deserve to feel that way. This way of dealing with feelings gives me *more* anxiety. I have found that I am a person that needs to sit in what's going on, even if I'm being told I don't deserve to feel that way.

I have a biological desire to be with my daughter a lot more than another mother may, and I'm going to honor that.

I am wired to take care of others' needs before mine, and I'm going to honor that.

When my daughter would cry, it broke my heart, and at times, I canceled my plans.

When the oxygen mask falls in the airplane (I know this is overused, but), I know my first instinct will be to put it on my daughter, and I honor that.

Do you miss your baby when you're at work? Honor that feeling.

Do you miss your colleagues and the work you did now that you're at home full time? Honor that.

Does a girlfriend getaway give you anxiety because you're still breast-feeding, and your husband is traveling until that Friday? *Honor how you are feeling in that moment.*

What gives me less anxiety is my decision to roll with the Mom Guilt instead of pushing it away. I still don't let it consume me or take over. Instead, I'm working hard (*really* hard) to be aware of what my feelings mean, acknowledge them, and figure out ways to not let them stop me from doing the things I want to do.

You want to know how I came to this mentality? As a children's author, I interact with children in schools and events with my books and their wellness themes. In my book, *I Can Conquer!* my main goal is to teach children about honoring one's fears and finding ways to work with them versus against them. It's interesting that through inspiring and educating children, I found a road that I actually needed to take as well. One important tool of the book I stress when I talk to children is that a fear may never go away. Conquering your fear simply means you *didn't let it stop you.*

The key is finding your confidence as a mom, but how?

You're doing an amazing job, and it's time you ACKNOWLEDGE this! I want you to list all the things you are rocking at as a mother. I'll help you out and list the first one:

1. You created and are keeping a human being alive

Now it's your turn! Start a list here, and if you can, try listing things on a daily basis. Even if it's a simple yellow PostIt note slapped on your fridge. Especially if you're having one of those days where you're being hard on yourself. It's easy to get swallowed up by the negative feelings. The sooner you are aware, acknowledge, and write things down, the sooner you're going to find solutions to work with these feelings instead of running from them. It's time to celebrate all you're doing, learning, and giving as a new mom.

Let's begin, and keep it simple:

2.

3.

4.

5.

If you have older children, or when your baby gets old enough, I want you to ask them what *they* love about you. I also want you to ask your partner/spouse the same question. You can do that right now! Write it all down and keep it close.

And at the end of the day ...

None of us know what we are doing.

In motherhood, there are no rules.

No one is the expert.

Create your own standards based on your family.

Guilt means different things to different mothers.

Don't blame yourself.

Don't punish yourself.

Don't withdraw.

Connect with "your people" to talk about these feelings.

Work with your feelings; don't tell them to fuck off.

Allow the feelings to create the desire to do something different next time.

And finally, at the end of the day, the Beatles had it right when they sang, "All you need is love." That's all your baby needs and will remember.

CHAPTER 7

Being a Mom Can Be
REALLY Boring!

Motherhood makes you feel like you're stranded on a deserted island like Tom Hanks in the movie *Castaway*. Your Wilson volleyball is your baby. You talk to your baby as if it's going to indulge in conversation. You shake things that rattle. Play endless rounds of peekaboo. Read ten books out loud. Sing "Wheels on the Bus" and expect a round of applause for your performance. You're desperate for any response.

You walk into your home as a new mom, and your maternity leave starts and perhaps never ends. Suddenly ten hours of your day are free for you to figure out what the F to do with your baby. Add in the couple hours where you used to grab drinks with friends. Now you have two more hours on your plate. Then the hour when you took a SoulCycle class and the hour you watched Bravo, and you have two more hours. Don't forget your baby is "awake" most of the hours when you used to be soundly sleeping. Oh yes, it's the after-hours party you wish you never showed up for.

82

Before baby, you accomplished great things in your career, learned new things every day, and interacted with interesting people. Today, motherhood seems to rob you of these personal accomplishments. You feel unsatisfied and ineffective even though you're exhausted and burnt out. It's difficult to justify your day when you're doing such mundane tasks. You're desperate to make this day a bit more exciting but is going back to work the only solution?

I created so much pressure and high expectations based on outside sources. One day it was from an article I read, then I'd tap on my Wonder Weeks app, and the next I'd fall down the rabbit hole of a Facebook group about all the things other moms were doing with their babies. Thank God I wasn't Pinterest-savvy. The guilt mounted in my brain if I wasn't paying attention to her, playing with her, teaching her, and creating for her. I was a chaotic clown at a circus, exhausted from being "on" all day.

The personal neglect also contributed to my boredom. I wasn't doing the things I loved to do before I became a mom. I still loved music, concerts, reading, exercising, being outdoors, traveling, art, restaurants, and binge-watching reality TV. I enjoyed getting dressed up, doing my hair, and wearing makeup. Ninety-minute yoga classes energized me. Long walks by the river inspired me. Every single one of these things was put on a bookshelf the moment I entered my home as a new mom. My day consisted of at least twenty hours of baby.

The days were so long. As the sun peeked through the shades, I looked up at the clock and immediately started the countdown. I would throw out twenty baby activities with Brooklyn, then look up at the clock to find only an hour had passed. Only twenty-three more hours to go!

The first few months I quarantined myself with Brooklyn. I exaggerate but it was pretty close. It was a horrible winter and flu season where I was afraid to bring Brooklyn out of the house. Then there was that darn diaper bag. Feelings of overwhelm took over when I even thought of packing

THE Honest Mom PROJECT

a diaper bag, all that needed to go in it, and all the things that could go wrong. I'd give up before even opening the door.

There is only so much you can do within the walls of your home before you start getting cabin fever and feel the need to escape. My deserted island was preventing me from becoming the mother I was meant to be. I didn't know how to escape. I didn't realize I had a choice.

The ultimate photobomb

I based all my baby activity expectations around photos, ads, and social media posts. Let's call it the Family Fantasy Filter. Bath time for example. It started with strolls down the aisles of Buy Buy Baby's bath section. Not only was I in a tunnel of bath toys galore, but I also noticed photos on the boxes of families splashing, laughing, and making it seem like this is how one should feel while washing a baby. There were bubbles, colors, squirty things, and babies who squealed with joy. Nowhere was a photo of the turd the baby released or the mom mindlessly staring at her baby as she struggled to keep her eyes open.

Well, I registered for a bunch of bath gear and continued to buy more gear with the hopes that the laughter and splashing would entertain me. To this day …

I still hate bath time.
It bores me to death.
I celebrated the day she could shower by herself.

What's really going on mom?

It's a massive adjustment when you take a break from an autonomous life filled with choices of excitement, fun, and personal growth. It's paralyzing when you're forced to embrace a life where you feel you've surrendered to something completely dependent upon you. Coming from a life where ten hours of your day are filled with your job to a day where ten hours are wide open can be mind-boggling. A life of interaction with interesting people, compared to a life with a baby that can't talk, can be isolating.

And boring! You feel you had a pre-baby life where you were learning and growing where now you're on a deserted island without a compass or map. Days can go by very slowly and you may find yourself constantly trying to find ways to entertain your baby. You don't enjoy many of the mom things that you're supposed to and no one else is talking about that so you keep silent.

What are you really missing and yearning for now that you're a mom? If you're like many women, it's pretty simple (and normal):

- You want connection. To your baby. To other moms.
  To anyone with a pulse.

- You want the adrenaline rushes of the past.
  Exciting risks and situations.

- You want to grow and become better each day
  to reach your full potential.

- And maybe there are just some things you
  truly don't enjoy doing.

Maybe you hate the infant stage like I did?

You may not enjoy a certain stage of your child's life. Some love newborns and are pregnant the moment their baby starts walking. Others have the best memories and laughter from toddlerhood; others call their children Cheech & Chong. I spoke with a mother that bravely admitted she didn't enjoy motherhood until her children were teenagers. Some find that the teen years are the worst.

I hated the infancy stage. I legit didn't enjoy it. Toddlerhood gave me some wonderful memories and hysterical videos, but it was still mentally and physically draining. The "magic" started when Brooklyn turned four and continues as a nine-year-old. I'm in love with the past five years and the closeness Brooklyn and I have. Our conversations, the adventures, and even the challenges have created a strong connection between us.

So if you're not enjoying this time, take a breath and know it's OK. This may be a stage that exhausts you in all ways. Frustration may take over any enjoyment of your days. You may be in survival mode and just want the day to end. Each stage of raising a child is challenging in different ways. On top of it, each child and parent are different from your family.

When it gets hard, I use a tool from Mel Robbins from her book, *The Five Second Rule*. I remove myself from the situation, take in a deep breath, and count down from five. I think of one thing that I appreciate in that moment. I breathe in again, counting down from five, and return. It's amazing how much clearer the skies are after that.

It doesn't help that we are creating this story

I have good news for you. You create the monotony and boredom in your life. Harsh statement, but it's also pretty powerful and freeing. When you take responsibility for creating a fulfilling life under your terms, you can get back the excitement, growth, and connection you desire. If you're bored playing in your house all day, then get out of your house. That's what I had to do, and I still do it. We are pressured to buy all this at home equipment to entertain our children where many times it traps us in our homes. I'm not someone that enjoys being in her home all day. I crave getting out with Brooklyn, going to museums, parks, our local Arboretum, a movie, the pool, or a day trip to the city. She gets stir-crazy too, so it works for the both of us.

Remember what you can control: The meaning behind everything, your reaction to it, the people you surround yourself with, and best of all, you control your definition of what fulfills you. It's your story to tell.

Figuring out your own reality

You've done three-hundred Google searches, but let's add one more. "What to do when you're bored being a mom." Enter. Your page floods with mommy blogs, *Huffington Post* articles, and *Parents* magazine articles. Each one you click on seem to have the same advice: create a routine, get out of the house, join a mommy group, do a mommy-and-me music class, find mom-friends, or go after that "side hustle."

Those last two words still make me cringe.

Listen, if any of those resonate with you that's great. If they don't, you need to figure out your own reality and what drives you down the right road. Give yourself some grace and patience as you do this because it's hard. I knew I needed to get out of the house, attempt baby-wearing more, and continue to do the things I loved. Nine years later, I wish I did. After all, that was the best time to do it. Brooklyn was immobile, couldn't talk, and therefore couldn't complain or have a meltdown. At the time, I felt way too selfish to even think of doing something that I enjoyed. I was a mom. It was all about her.

There was too much guilt and anxiety when I attempted to do something that I wanted to do. I had a swarm of "What Ifs" that I created in my head with every single situation I dreamt of:

- What if I hired a nanny and I miss out on something she does?

- What if I hired a nanny and she neglects Brooklyn? What if I catch something on a nanny-cam?!

- What if I wanted to get a cup of coffee and read, and my husband thinks I'm lazy?

- What if my business grows so much that I don't spend any time with her?

- What if I take her with me and she starts crying?

- What if I breastfeed in public and someone scolds me?

- What if I put her in the baby-wrap and she starts crying and won't stop?

- What if I shower and she rolls out of her bouncy seat? Even though she's one-month old and strapped in?

- What if she cries too long and her brain gets damaged?

- What if she can remember me being gone for too long?

- What if she blows out all her diapers and I have a baby full of poo and don't have anything to change her into?

- What if she won't take a bottle and starves?

- What if she doesn't nap for my mom? She'll only fall asleep to the boob!

- What if my husband doesn't know what to do but is afraid to call me? Or what if he does call me forty-seven times?

I've gained confidence and eased the anxiety through time and with the people I connected with to ease my anxiety. If only I had connected with these people sooner, this healing would have gone a lot faster. One person that started the momentum was Brooklyn's nanny. Before Sally's first day, I sent her a six-page Word document outlining Brooklyn's day down to the minute. Along with the schedule, detailed descriptions about each activity, feeding, nap, and possible behavior. When Sally showed up (I can't believe she did after what I sent her), she respectfully had the printout in her hand and said something like, "Oh, now this gave me a chuckle."

Sally had a lot of experience paired with a vibrant personality. She was also very honest. At times, I felt she was my nanny as well! After I'd get home from work, Sally and I would catch up at my kitchen island about Brooklyn and life in general. She'd tell her stories of motherhood and I'd ask questions, eager to learn. Without judgment, our conversations created so much comfort and slowly I started becoming more confident in what I was doing. I wanted her advice, her stories, along with her reassuring, "I did my best and that's good enough" closings to those stories. I needed Sally for more than just caring for Brooklyn while I was away. The trust that I found in her gave me the courage to go out and find others to talk to as well.

My role with Brooklyn was to love her, feed her, and keep her safe. All those things could have been accomplished while I was enjoying new restaurants, going on walks along the river, listening to an outdoor concert, or meeting up with friends for coffee. I wasn't in tune with my reality. I was living by expectations that weren't even mine. I created anxiety with all the what ifs that never ended up happening. I made decisions based on guilt and what was easy, versus working toward happiness as an individual. To become the mother I was meant to be, I had to honor *my* needs as well as my daughter's. Thankfully I found the right people to ignite the light and create the confidence to do this.

Get out of your boredom by creating their boredom

"Boredom-busting ideas for kids"
"Twenty simple ways to entertain your child"
"How do I keep my child entertained for hours?"

These are just three of the thousands of Google and Pinterest searches that moms do when they're pulling their hair out for ideas. I couldn't even read past these eight:

1. Write your own story.
2. Put on a play.
3. Do an art challenge.
4. Make Play-Doh sculptures and put on an art show.
5. Create a gratitude or vision board.
6. Draw murals outside with colored chalk.
7. Collect rocks and paint them.
8. Create chalk dolls and dress them up.

If all of these make you say "Awww" and you can't wait to get all your supplies, that's great and you can skip this section. But if you're rolling your eyes or having a Pinterest anxiety attack, read on. The expectation to create a circus around our children has got to stop so we can get our sanity back. Our lives! Oh, I was there, and still have to remind myself to step back.

Thank God for Brooklyn's teachers throughout her first four years of life. They were all extensions of our family and raising Brooklyn. One of the most important lessons they taught me was the lesson of independent play and allowing her to figure out her world on her own. It's hard to do though. The mom guilt can swallow you. You'll hear the voices in your head saying,

- "You're not helping enough,"
- "You're not paying enough attention to him,"
- "She's not learning what others are, so you need to get those flashcards out,"
- "Oh jeez, he looks bored and is whining for me, let me run and go save the day!"
- What I didn't know? **It's good for them to be bored.**

When we step back and give our children some breathing room, it's incredible what they can discover. As an infant, you don't have to stimulate them for hours. Set them down on their tummies and let them move, observe, take in, and enjoy what's around them. When your child is a toddler, you can put their toys on shelves of their height so they can freely choose what they want to do. Then step back and give them space to enjoy in their own way. It's also so interesting to watch from the sidelines. Now that Brooklyn is nine, she knows that if I have to make dinner or if she needs some quiet time after getting off the bus, she can go to her areas and do her thing.

Being bored is good for your child. Constant entertainment and stimulation in their face doesn't give room for them to figure out their own fun. Dr. Alison Escalante, MD, is a pediatrician and told *Psychology Today*, "The first barrier to our kids' boredomtunities is us. The obvious reasons are that we hate their whining, we find their unhappiness very hard to tolerate, and sometimes we just need to get something done." She then talks about the benefits of boredom, citing a piece that Jude Stewart wrote about the benefits of boredom: Igniting creativity, independence, coping skills, problem solving, and just allowing one to discover the world on their own. When we constantly entertain our children, toss a device at them any time they whine, or sign them up for a slew of activities just to keep them occupied, they can't develop these skills.

You want your child to be independent and take pride in creating their own joy. Just like you want that for yourself. Alleviate the stress and exhaustion so you can make room for things you want to do. Start practicing this in the infancy and toddler stage so your children can thrive in this world without expecting the outside world to do it for them!

It's time to opt-out, or at least delegate!

Thanks to a podcast episode of *What Fresh Hell,* I learned how to bring the topic of "opting out" into motherhood. When we can opt out of annoying emails, why not annoying tasks or activities you just don't want to deal with? What else do I wish I could "opt out" of? Well, let's see ...

Anything that has to do with pretending to be something.

Schoolwork at home. I never enjoyed doing homework or summer schoolwork with my mom either.

Dress up. Enough said.

Spa day. No thank you to *Fancy Nancy* and her "Oooh La La Spa"!

Bath time. I have always, and continue, to hate bath time.

Playing in our basement. I hate our basement. It's one room in my home that doesn't give me good energy. I think I have some sort of PTSD from constantly going there when she was a toddler. I'd just stare at Brooklyn as she played with our exercise equipment and other random toys. It's also the area of pretend play as the costumes are down there. Simply put, it's not my happy place.

Going to the park. Now that she's older, I'm enjoying it more. When she was a toddler, I had total anxiety about her falling fifteen feet through the eight different random open areas. Who designs these jungle gyms anyways?! When she was a toddler, my husband or I would be climbing the equipment with her because there were always older kids running and pushing others around. It was just filled with anxiety for me. Now that she's older, it's still not the best and most entertaining for me, but it's tolerable.

There were so many things that believed I had to enjoy to qualify as a fun mom. A good mom. Not only did I feel guilty for not enjoying every single moment with my daughter, but I also didn't hear other moms talk about the things they didn't enjoy. I basically felt like I was either complaining or inadequate with finding joy in the things Brooklyn and I were doing. Until I realized I wasn't going to enjoy *everything*, and didn't have to, I was going to be bored and unhappy. Instead, I should have delegated or opted out of them so I could make space for the things I loved. To find my own joy.

I'm here to tell you it's not selfish to expose your child to the things that *you* enjoy. It's a gift. And yes, there were times when I had to give her a bath. But there are other times I simply tell her I'm just not in the mood to do what she wants in that moment. She then learns that it's not all about her, which helps her in life and her relationships.

David Code, a family therapist and author of *To Raise Happy Kids, Put Your Marriage First,* writes about how our over-focus of putting our children first is doing more damage than we realize:

"Today's number one myth about parenting is that the more attention we give our kids, the better they'll turn out. But we parents have gone too far: our over-focus on our children is doing them more harm than good. Families centered on children create anxious, exhausted parents, and demanding, entitled children. We parents are too quick to sacrifice our lives and our marriages for our kids. Most of us have created child-centered families, where our children hold priority over our time, energy, and attention."

In my eyes, teaching your child that life isn't always about them is one of the best gifts you can give them. Sure, it's important that they know they are important, and there are certain situations where it is all about them. But not all the time. They also need to know what's important to you so they can get to know you beyond being their mother. You have permission to honor your passions, teach your children about the give-take world, and stop feeling like you're not a good parent if you don't like playing Ninja Princess.

What are you going to opt out of starting right now? Who could you delegate it to? What would you like to do instead? It's time to find joy in your days.

I'm going to opt out of:	Delegate it to:	Instead, I'd like to:
Example: Mommy & Me Music Class	*Grandma!*	*Take her to the park*

"Your dreams do not have to make you famous to matter."

—Monica Packer of the About Progress podcast

There is no rule that says you must let go of your dreams, passions, and interests because of your new life as a mother. I see this pressure out there for moms to be Instagram-famous or make six-figures with their dreams. I felt it myself. Why can't we learn something new, take a class, join a group, read, write, and create without the pressure of conquering the world or making money?

When I read Elizabeth Gilbert's book, *Big Magic*, I finally calmed my anxiety to attach status and financial goals to my creativity. Like you, I love to learn and feel like every day I'm growing as a person. When I became a mother, for some reason, I felt that for my dreams to be important or have value, they had to have this status attached to them. I had to be contributing financially or it was a waste of my time.

With learning, growing, and being creative, the pressure to make it a business or reach a number of followers on Instagram began to suffocate me. I was passionate about wellness but was told I couldn't just share my knowledge with others. I needed to make money, or I was being taken advantage of. I loved writing but instead of keeping it for myself, I felt pressure to create a blog and be "professional" about it. As a result, what I thrived on and enjoyed weren't feeding my soul like they used to. They eventually turned into responsibilities and achievements of other people's expectations. I felt overwhelmed where instead my creativity should have been my outlet.

Then this book was born. Obviously, I love to write. I love to share my experiences and what I've learned. I also love to help people. These three things became the purpose and motivation behind this book. Of course, I wouldn't mind if it became a *NYT* best-seller, let's be honest, but this time I'm not putting the pressures upon myself like I used to. I've chosen to honor what fuels me and connects me with others. What will allow me to grow and thrive off my creativity.

It's time for you to find things to call your own and fuel your insides with excitement, pride, information, interesting people, delight, culture, and anything else that gives you the growth you desire. Take a class and don't worry about becoming the expert in something. Read a book simply to learn and be inspired. Watch a documentary you're interested in or engage in an interesting conversation with someone. There's an interesting person inside of you. Finding her will ignite confidence to create an even more amazing mother and inspiration to your family.

Someone failed to mention ...

- My daughter needed time on her own and that it was beneficial to her.

- I needed time on my own as well.

- I'm a good mom even if my child is bored.

- I may not enjoy every stage in her development.

- It's OK if I don't enjoy certain activities.

- I can opt-out or delegate things to other people and do things I enjoy.

- I can still follow my passions without making them a career.

- It's not a waste of time to have hobbies and things outside being a mom.

And at the end of the day ...

It's not all shit's creek, but it's also not all rainbows, unicorns, and roses. The dialogue between moms needs to change where we are comfortable admitting when things suck, and it doesn't qualify our level of motherhood. You can safely say, "God, I can't stand tummy time; what the hell am I supposed to do while she lays on her stomach for ten minutes?" Maybe you've been in your house with a snowstorm and find yourself more entertained staring out the window, wishing the hands on the clock would go just a little bit faster? Perhaps you're at a mommy-and-me music class at the local park district with a bunch of moms you have no connection with as you realize you're only there to pass an hour of time?

It's OK to be honest about these feelings and say them out loud. You're also talking about the things you are enjoying to mix it up and create a real story of motherhood. And that story will be pretty darn interesting. Regardless of the MOM stamp, you're not going to enjoy every single moment. Just like you don't enjoy every single moment of other parts of your life. To break the monotony and boredom, you first need to find that map and compass and get off your deserted island. There's so much out there for you to discover. You deserve it.

CHAPTER 8

Why Wasn't I Invited
to the Party?

It's 2 a.m. and pitch black in my daughter's room. I rock back and forth in my glider as I nurse her with one arm and flick my thumb down, down, down the rabbit hole.

I pause on a perfectly filtered photo of a table of my friends holding up their fun and colorful cocktails as the caption reads, "Cheers to a night out away from the kiddos!"

I wake to feed her at 5 a.m., and as I open Facebook again, another group of friends pop in my face at a wedding I should have been at. They're dressed to the nines as I sit in what I loosely call my pajamas I've been in for two days. My thumb continues to whip my screen back down the rabbit hole where I pause on a shot of my colleagues going to our favorite restaurant in the city as I sit on my brown couch on maternity leave in the suburbs. The daily news at its finest.

From a social butterfly to the land of FOMO

Before Brooklyn, I was not only a social butterfly, but I was also a social hummingbird, bumblebee, and whatever flying object skirts from one thing to the next. Always an extrovert, I thrived off meeting new people, getting to know friends even better, and making some incredible memories.

It was hard for me to sit at home. I felt like I was missing out on something. Plus, I lived in an area of the city where there was action no matter what corner you turned. For the most part, I was always doing something with someone. There were college friends, grade school friends, and work friends that surrounded me where a text with an invitation to hang out was always accepted.

It was more challenging than I had thought to move to the suburbs, away from the city, the action, and my friends. Even though I was still working in the city, it was getting more challenging to keep my social life active there. The commute was a bear and took its toll as I'd miss one train and groan when I realized the next one wasn't leaving for another hour. I'd have dinner alongside a bout of anxiety as I looked at my watch to gauge when I'd need to hail a cab to the train station. Many times, I'd arrive home after 11 p.m. with a 4:30 a.m. wakeup call the next morning to head back to the city for work. It was getting really old, and I was quickly growing tired of it all.

Once I had Brooklyn, that's when my FOMO (Fear of Missing Out) was created and festered. It brewed daily and at times bubbled over. Of course, I was missing out on things as a new mom. Shouldn't that have been obvious to me? How could this NOT happen as I sat in my family room all damn day and night with a baby suctioned on my boob?

What was even harder was the fact that I had Brooklyn later in life where I was in a completely different stage than my friends. Most had been back in action, returned to their full-time careers with lives adjusted to their new normal. What sucked is I felt I was just getting started—and doing it all alone.

Ironically, I chose to do something that actually created even more loneliness. To protect my ego, I began to isolate myself from my friends. I created a mindset that isolation was safe for me and avoided things becoming *more* complicated than they already were. It was too difficult to leave the house. It was hard enough to simply shower. Even harder to imagine getting dressed, put on makeup, curl my hair, and attempt to pull denim up my lower half. Known as the "life of the party," I couldn't admit that I didn't want to go anywhere.

Sure, I responded to texts asking, "How are you doing?" where I always seemed to respond with, "I'm fine." The first couple weeks were filled with visits from friends and other family members wanting to meet Brooklyn. My mom came to help a lot, or to simply keep me company. It wasn't as if I was in a dark room in solitary confinement with my daughter. After a while though, I wasn't seeing anyone but my husband, my mom, and Brooklyn. There's only so much asking and reaching out my friends could do, right?

At some point, I had to bring something to the table. What stopped me were all the bottled-up emotions I held inside when it came to leaving Brooklyn. I told myself breastfeeding was holding me captive. I allowed my mom guilt of abandoning her control my decisions. There was too much to explain with her nighttime routine, so it was easier to just stay.

Sadly, I also felt that as an individual, I didn't have anything to offer at that time. I was a zombie, barely sleeping, and the start of each day made me feel like I was in the repetitive scene of *Groundhog Day* with Bill Murray's alarm going off at 6:00 a.m. playing Sonny and Cher's "I Got You Babe."

It sounded like a good idea at the time

I took the bull by the horns and organized a dinner at a swanky and hip restaurant in the city. All but one of my friends had kids that were beyond the newborn stage. They had sitters established or husbands who were able to feed their children without a breast. I decided to bring Brooklyn since some of my friends hadn't met her yet. She slept on the ride to the city, I put her on the boob and fed her quickly in the parking garage and headed to the restaurant with her stroller and monster diaper bag.

I can do this. I am doing this.

I approach the entrance to the restaurant and notice there is a six-foot-something bouncer at the door in a tight black shirt, even tighter pants, and I handed him my ID and questioned inside, "A bouncer? At 6 o'clock on a Tuesday?"

Parting the Red Sea of twenty-somethings with my bright red stroller, I was surrounded by an after-work crowd with cocktails, cleavage, and self-ies. Club music provided by a DJ was thumping as I searched for my friends. But the only song that played in my head was Sesame Street's "One of These Things" where I felt I was the one that didn't belong.

I checked my stroller and awkwardly carried the ungodly heavy car seat as I struggled to wave at the booth that contained my friends. Brooklyn and I were greeted with big smiles, hugs, and shouts of, "Oh my God, she's beautiful!" over the club music as we sat down to catch up.

I said I got this, right? Piece of cake.

But about twenty minutes into the dinner, Brooklyn was done. She was not entertained by the loud music; she hated being in her car seat; she hated when my friends held her; she hated when I held her, and I wasn't comfortable with breastfeeding in a club full of twenty-somethings taking selfies with me in the background. (Ask me what I'd do today, and I'd say FUCK IT!)

I drove home defeated in tears. Not only did I feel I wasn't invited to the party, but I couldn't even throw my own party without motherhood getting in the way. The deserted island I was so desperate to escape was slowly becoming my retreat.

Take a breath, and take it slowly

Take small steps.

You don't have to go-go-go to prove you're connected to the outside world.

Don't overwhelm yourself or do things you're not ready for.

Start with coffee.

It's just like dating.

You wouldn't have a five-hundred-person wedding on your first date, so why shouldn't your first mom-outing be the same?

What's really going on, Mom?

I don't know about you, but I believe that as human beings we have cravings beyond sex and a bag of Doritos. We, as humans, also have emotional cravings. We yearn to feel loved, to feel wanted, appreciated, validated, and included. I've talked about this need in other chapters: the need for CONNECTION. As much as I crave some time to myself, I'm also not wired to be completely alone. I desire to be a part of something, to be in a community, to have experiences that I create and am invited to. When we become mothers, that connection is needed even more in order for us to grow. The problem is, we are moving farther away from it than ever before.

You don't live next door to your mom or down the street from your sister. Your best friends don't live in the same neighborhood as you all grew up in. Face-to-face connection has changed throughout the decades, and as a new mom, now is the time you need it the most. Texts and Facebook posts aren't the same. Mommy Facebook groups where you've found amazing moms in the same boat helps, but it doesn't give you everything you need. How can you change this as you sit on your deserted island with your baby?

Put the plug into the outlet

Get some real *live* connections.

Nothing beats an old-school face to face gathering.

Find something at your local church, MOPS group,
or ask your hospital what groups you can join.

"Are we conditioned to feel insecure or disappointed if we think we miss an opportunity that others have made the most of?"
(From episode 73 of the Coffee + Crumbs podcast)

Are we making up stories about what we are missing or a life that we've never experienced? Is the grass really greener? Moms are professionals at creating their own versions of reality inside their head. I am one of the biggest storytellers out there. If I learned of a gathering of friends or a double date in my circle, I'd immediately create a story. One story was that I was boring and that's why I wasn't included. Another story was my life was inconvenient for them. They assumed I didn't want to go. I'd write a story that my friends' husbands thought my husband was boring. My story would become more elaborate the longer I obsessed about it. Before I knew it, I came to the general conclusion that no one wanted to hang out with me. Otherwise, they would ask me to join them, right?

The negative storytelling was also about me as a person. My beliefs, and what I would tell myself daily, were all centered on the lack of confidence

I had in myself. No one was telling me I was boring. I was. I've never had a friend tell me my husband is boring. I just assumed that. My husband never said I was unattractive. I told myself that. I believed the story that people were intentionally leaving me out. The stories in my head also created the story I told to the world around me. As a result, I was attracting just what I asked for. Nothing.

Who is to blame for my insecurities? Well, I could blame social media, as it seemed to be my only connection to what others were doing. It's not like my friends were texting me photos with, "Having so much fun without you!" I wasn't getting an invitation in the mail to a party with the words, "You're NOT invited!" Did social media instigate some feelings? Absolutely.

Still, the roots to my insecurities were already inside of me. I needed to dig out of that dirt and find the confidence in the life I was living so I could scroll in a healthier way. We'll be talking more about social media and its effects on us as mothers soon, so stay tuned.

Cut to the chase

Get your voice out and communicate with your friends to let them know how you feel. It's the only way to figure out what's really going on to gain some reassurance with your friendships. You may be surprised at what they tell you!

Living as an outsider
instead of an insider

Life as a new mom can feel a bit monotonous and boring. I get it. That was part of the reason I lived my life in FOMO-land. I spent most of my time living in other people's worlds instead of my own. I'd compare and base my life off of a two-second photo in the tens of millions of seconds of a year. To top it off, you're only getting about two percent of the real story in that photo.

The power of media to influence huge decisions in life, emotions, and values can be dangerous. Social media has become a platform for bragging where we've passed the torch to anyone that has a smartphone, giving you small, sometimes inaccurate, snippets that create heightened emotions and disconnect you from what truly makes you secure in your life.

UN-socialize your media

Take a social media break.

How do you feel when you're on social media scrolling away?

If it's continuing to make or you can't seem to monitor it in a healthy way, a short break may be in order.

When you return, find people that make your heart full and stay up to date on them.

Instead of mindlessly scrolling, be intentional with social media.

We can't just drop and go like we used to

Moms definitely earn the URGENT badge when they raise children. Everything is urgent. We live in urgency and get blasted with last minute changes or hiccups. Kids get the stomach flu, naps can hold us hostage, sitters cancel, and spouses travel plans change at the last minute. There are just some days where you're thrown into the ring one too many times. Suddenly you're too damn exhausted to even think about leaving your house.

Do we look at our child as the one holding us hostage? Honestly, I did at times.

- I was frustrated because it was so difficult to leave her while she was breastfeeding.

- Resentful when she kept me up all night and I was so miserably tired I canceled plans.

- Angry that something this little could control so many decisions in my day.

I missed the days where I'd get a text and all I had to do was hop in a cab to get there. Back in the day, nothing made me tired, depressed, guilty, overwhelmed, or full of anxiety to do the things I wanted to do. Now I was in a world where I felt I wasn't in control of my life. The more I allowed this, the more I isolated myself on my deserted island with a big case of FOMO.

Take the FOMO quiz

This in no way is to give you a formal diagnosis, just a simple quiz to get you out of the fog and a bit more in tune with your feelings. Be honest and know that once you acknowledge your feelings, you can start making changes. Total your answers at the end and see where your level of FOMO is right now (not forever!).

1. How often do you check social media throughout the day?

   1: Obsessively
   2: Periodically (maybe a few times a day for short periods
   3: Once a day, if at all

2. Do you have the need to know what your friends are doing most of the time?

   1: Always
   2: Somewhat
   3: Rarely

3. It's Saturday night; you're at home and no one has texted you. Do you feel:

    1: Paranoid and wonder what's going on

    2: A bit bummed out

    3: You're fine and are doing something you want to do

4. Your friends are planning a girls' trip, and you can't go this time. Do you feel:

    1: Depressed and constantly think about all you'll miss

    2: You keep thinking of ways it can work.
    You're not going down without a fight!

    3: Disappointed but there will be another one
    once your boobs aren't on duty

5. You're scrolling through Instagram and see your friends all decked out with cocktails in their hands, probably clinking to a "CHEERS TO NO KIDS!" Do you feel:

    1: Instant jealousy

    2: You wish you were there but will get over it

    3: Happy for them

Now that you've been completely honest about your FOMO, add up your numbers and write the total down here: _____. 15 is on the high end of the FOMO scale and 5 is the low end, and based on where your score falls, you have an idea of your level. If you're closer to 5, I'm so happy for you and hope this will continue. But if you're heading toward 15 or already there, there's some work to be done.

Be proud of your honesty because it's the only way to climb that ladder and get to the top. You're a work in progress, like so many other moms out there.

Sometimes you are missing out, and that's just the way it is

The sooner we acknowledge the season of life we're in, the sooner we will accept the life we're in at that moment. When I look back to when my FOMO was at its peak, there was *no way* I was able to do some of the things my friends were doing. Nor did I want to do them. There's beauty in simple answers to make acceptance a bit easier. Acceptance will allow you to plug into your life of today, heal, and start your own journey.

> You're just going to miss out on some things right now.
> That's OK.
> I promise it won't last forever.

Next time you're scrolling

1. People are allowed to have fun without you.

2. Next time you're on social media, be happy for your friends.

3. Change the wording in your mind to "I'm really happy they got to go out without their kids," "I'm happy they had a date night," or "I'm really happy they are having so much fun."

4. Final step: comment on the social media post with positive words.

A simple word can change it all

I'm a huge Marie Forleo fan and incorporate so many of her teachings and tools into motherhood. One technique from her latest book, *Everything is Figureoutable,* is changing the word "can't" to "won't." I was a bit skeptical at first, something so simple changing your mindset so drastically. Then I did the exercise.

Next time you say inside, "Ugh, I *can't* go back to work now; I just feel I want to be at home right now," change it to, "I *won't* go back to work now; I want to be at home with my daughter." Instead of, "I *can't* drive three hours to our family reunion where we'll either have to share a bedroom or get a hotel," change it to, "I *won't* be going to the family reunion because it just isn't in the cards this year." Changing your mindset from "I *can't*" to "I won't" creates acknowledgment, then acceptance, and gives you power to pivot in the right direction.

Have patience with your new life and your recovery

Instead of feeling sorry for yourself (you're allowed to do it just a bit—but not forever), take *pride* in recovering after having a baby. Not only is your body recovering, but you're also an entirely different person and there's some adjustment that needs time and TLC.

There's so much pressure to "get your body back," "get your life back," "get yourself back," where I wonder why are we running from where we're at in life? Why are we constantly looking back or searching for a future that we make up in our heads? Take a moment to breathe and just be in your life, your present life, for the time being. Rest. Take care of your baby. Be gentle to your body and your spirit. Don't add on any new pressures or anxieties just because you're feeling you're supposed to be doing something else. You're not. You're right where you need to be.

"Good for her, not for me."
—Amy Poehler

My friends and I were planning a girls' trip. Dates started to solidify, flight costs were being shared, where suddenly one of our friends fell silent from the group texts. Eventually she said, "Girls, I don't think I can make this happen."

She just had a baby, was exclusively breastfeeding around the clock, her husband traveled Monday through Friday, she had two other girls under the age of six, and unreliable childcare. We had a "Come to Jesus" moment with her and told her anything that gave her that much anxiety was anything but self-care. What's crazy is I'm writing this a year later and this past year has flown by so fast. She's at an entirely different stage in life and is ready to plan the next trip. She was brave to be honest with us and knew we'd support her.

Like my friend, you need to be real about what you really want to be doing *right now*, in the season of life you're in *right now*. What will work versus what will be chaotic and stressful. Having clear goals doesn't just apply to a career, it goes for your entire life. You must do the work to gain the confidence in what you want to do, versus what you think you should do.

Don't look at her life, or that mom's life, or even your sister's. You are a unique person who has a life that is different from everyone else's. No one else has the answers but you. I want you to pause, close this book, and think about what you truly want. Write it down on paper and save it. Heck, write it down in this book right now in the margin. Then when someone is posting about all they're doing in their life, and it doesn't ring true to yours, you can boldly say, "Good for her, not for me."

Ways to connect with friends versus waiting

We can all agree that waiting isn't going to get you anywhere so how will YOU connect with your friends to let them know you miss them? If you're stumped, here are some ideas to get you started:

1. An actual phone call. Set down the pride and pick up the phone. No texting allowed.

2. Send a funny card. Just because.

3. Send a half birthday card as a surprise.

4. Create a three-minute video of you saying hello and anything else you'd like to tell her.

5. Send a voice message versus a text message.

6. Mail a written invitation to coffee.

7. Leave a thoughtful gift at her doorstep.

8. Ask her if you can bring lunch to her office.

9. Mail her a postcard from a place you'd like to eventually go with her—and set a date!

Nothing is permanent

I tend to get in the mindset that what is going on in that moment is how it will be forever. When I sat in my home, day after day, night after night, it felt as if this was going to be my forever. I couldn't identify with anything other than what I was living. It's how Brooklyn sees just one moment of her day. I have to remind her how nothing is permanent, and every day is a new day. Each morning brings new situations, intentions, decisions, feelings and results your way. What you're going through today may not be what you experience tomorrow. Being united with the present is important, but there is also that link to the possibilities of the future. With some hope attached to it.

For today, honor how you feel but know nothing is permanent, and you will find the strength to change it. I return to my "Power of Yet" exercise that Brooklyn's kindergarten teacher ingrained in their brains. Anytime an event pops up, a promotion opportunity is thrown your way, or you casually find out that your friends did something without you, your response can be, "I'm not able to do that ... YET!"

CHAPTER 9

Hey, Where the Hell Did Everyone Go?!

"Just because you lost me as a friend, doesn't mean you gained me as an enemy." —*Tupac Shakur*

As early as preschool, your first "tribe" surrounds you. The walls of the classroom create your first versions of friendship, which usually include hitting, pinching, screaming, constant runny noses, pink eye, hand-foot-and-mouth and the rest of the daycare STDs. The next stage is kindergarten where you pretty much start over and like preschool, the walls keep you conveniently connected to your friends.

Each year you have the chance of not being in the same classroom as your best friend, but chances are if you're not, a recess or play date can keep things going. On to middle school, friendships become stronger but so do the cliques and divisions. Friends you once cherished throughout elementary school may now be "nerds," "the in-crowd," "weird," "quiet," and a handful of other labels kids create to alienate. In high school, your circle widens and depends on who you're dating, if you're on the volleyball team, cheerleading, or perhaps the theater.

If you venture off to college, you may leave some of the closest friends you'll ever have. Hopefully the connection is strong enough that you'll visit one another and spend plenty of time on breaks catching up. In college, your dorm surrounds you with potential friends right outside your door. If you're lucky, you may even like your roommate and gain a friend adjusting just like you are, even if only for that year. You decide to rush a sorority. There's yet another opportunity to be surrounded by a mountain of girl-friends, parties, group meals, formal events, study groups, Netflix binging, and simply having someone to always talk to.

When those years of college are over, and you head out to that big bright world, that's when friendships stand another test of survival. Marriage, moving, and new journeys ignite a bit of distance but then the big dog hits. Motherhood.

Loneliness is the enemy of motherhood

Humans, especially moms, need COMPANIONSHIP and CONNECTION for survival. No matter what you tell yourself, you're not wired to do this mom gig alone. I speak from experience and can confidently say: it's *impossible* to do it on your own. You may be thinking that if you can't "handle" motherhood that you're weak, incapable or (gasp!) a failure. I promise you, when you build that community around you, you become the strongest woman you've ever been. There's no prize for doing this on your own. There's no one to cheer you on. You don't have the resources, support, love, and much needed laughter that you desperately need. Loneliness and iso-lation will destroy the mother that you are meant to be. The mother you deserve to be.

Having a baby will change your friendships. Period.

Motherhood can challenge the friendships more than you expected. These women have been your friends for eons after all. Some were your brides-maids. Others you've known since you've were five years old. These strong friendships have stood the test of time. Unfortunately, time is probably the weakest link in the chain that holds your friendships together.

Your friendships can change in many ways. Not necessarily in a negative way. You may find some friendships becoming even stronger than they were before you became a mom. These are the ones to cherish and give extra work to. These friendships not only stand the test of time, but all the other crap that gets thrown our way once we become moms.

The struggles are real

No one told me how hard it would be to maintain an old friendship as a mother as well as create a new one. Nor was I given any head's up that I would have to let some friends go. I wasn't prepared for the fact that there would be friends that would be perfectly fine saying goodbye. Or flat out ghosting me.

Everyone is busy. Add a baby into the mix, and there's even less time to give. Many of your friends went back to work full-time. After they get home at 6 p.m., make dinner, have time with their kids, conduct the bed-time routine circus, they can't imagine doing anything else but putting on their pajamas. They're too damn exhausted to get together on a Tuesday night. Weekends are filled with soccer, dance, Costco, and Target trips. Not to mention fitting in anything they missed throughout the week.

Maybe you have a friend whose three kids are a bit older and involved in every extracurricular activity in the park district catalogue? In this case, you have a friend who is living out of her minivan without the time to even make a meal, much more hang with you.

Then there's the friend that you couldn't imagine losing, but rarely does she reach out to you. Not even a simple, "How's it going?" text message. She replies to your messages with brief, "Things are great!" but doesn't go into detail. Then you don't hear from her for months, if at all. You both used to talk every day. Drinks weekly. Girlfriend getaways every year. You knew every detail of one other's lives. Now you feel like she doesn't care if you ever talk again. She's becoming a stranger to you.

I don't think we realize all the different seasons in motherhood there are and how it can affect friendships when you're not in the same season. I'm sure you can agree that the newborn stage is different than the toddler stage and the elementary school stage is different than the high school stage. If you don't, that's OK; I didn't realize this until Brooklyn was getting older and I saw how my life changed with each season she and I traveled through. You may also find that you're a different person at different stages in your life.

Do you want to know what my two top challenges are with my friendships as a mother? The first is MY expectations of the friendship. Here we go again with me being in control of my life and happiness, right? My second obstacle? Holding on to the friendship for the wrong reason.

I'm SO busy!

I'm so bored and tired of "I'm so busy!" when I ask a friend how she's doing. I need more. This habitual response is creating distance between friends along with prevention of making new ones. I can't connect with the word "busy" anymore. Everyone's busy.

If a friend is too busy to make time for you, then I hate to break it to you, but you're not a priority for them. Like my mom says, life is about choices. We choose to overschedule our kids and live out of our cars. We choose to fill our day with fluff instead of creating space for what's import-ant. We choose not to call a friend. We choose to go to our child's thirtieth baseball game of the season over grabbing coffee with a friend we haven't seen in months. We choose to stay home and say fuck it versus making the effort to get ready to see friends for dinner. (BTW, I'm guilty of all of these.)

We all get the same twenty-four hours in a day. You choose how to fill them. If a friendship is important to you, you will carve out time for that friend. What do you need to get rid of to make that space? Because you have a lot more fluff than you realize.

Social media scrolling? Emails? Netflix binges? Sleeping in? Spending time with people that aren't as important as your dearest friends? You don't have to give up anything completely but check your screen time and if you have over thirty minutes a day, you have time for a friend. Instead of binge-watching Netflix for two hours on a Sunday, watch an hour and phone a friend the next hour. Sleep in for a bit but take a thirty-minute walk with a friend on a Saturday. It's all about priorities.

Seasons change, friendships change

Recognize that you may be an entirely different person based on the season of life you're in. Your friend may be as well. You both may not be a match at this time. You may have a friend doesn't have children, and this can affect your friendship.

I had a friend who chose not to have children and has built an amaz-ing career where she travels constantly, and when she's home, she's build-ing that business to match her dreams. Her life is amazing and fulfilled in different ways with different demands than mine. Sometimes these friend-ships can survive, but ours didn't align with her schedule along with what we even had in common anymore.

Only now do I realize that this is *perfectly* normal, and although it can be sad, friends may only be in your life for a certain part of it. They may not travel with you to the next stage, and you may not want to travel to theirs. Priorities change, time is taken even more than before, values change, and efforts change.

Maybe you come back together at a different time in life, and maybe you won't. Regardless of what happens, honor the friendship, be proud of it, and what you gained during that season.

"Expectation is the root of all heartache."
—William Shakespeare

I plugged in my ear buds with Jay Shetty's *On Purpose* podcast and listened to his episode titled "7 Signs You Need to Let Go of a Relationship & 6 Steps to Finally Break it Off." When he spoke about our expectations of a relationship versus their expectations, I acknowledged my biggest challenge with my troubled friendships.

My expectations were completely unrealistic, based on what I wanted to hold on to versus what I should have been in tune with.

Acknowledging this has been unbelievably freeing and life-changing. I finally was brave enough to admit that my expectations of the friendships were based on what our lives were like fifteen to twenty years ago. We were in college, then living together in the city, with no responsibilities other than ourselves. Simple responsibilities like showing up for work, paying our bills, eating, drinking, and sleeping.

During this time, one of our top three priorities was our friendship. There were no obstacles. No one had a sick child, a weekend-long soccer tournament, a day's worth of errands to run, a spouse who traveled that week, or felt guilty because she had been working a lot. My friends weren't running on three hours of sleep because they were up all night with their baby. They weren't utterly exhausted both physically and mentally. My friends had different lives and were different people back then. So was I.

If you remember from this book's first chapter, "If I Could Turn Back Time," I have a hard time of letting go of the past. I cling on to what was instead of acknowledging what is. My expectations of my friendships had to change for me to release the frustration, hurt, and at times anger. I needed to have a real conversation about the expectations my friends had of our friendship and what they could give based on their current lives. Until you do that, you will never be in sync and only create growing resentment inside you.

#friendshipgoals

It's time to set some goals of your own when it comes to friendships. You're a brand-new person, in an entirely different life, and you need to reevaluate what you require in a friendship as of TODAY. The drinking buddy from college who held your hair back may not be what you need in this stage of life you're in. The casual coworker that you'd grab dinner with every week and talk shop with may not be in the cards for your new life. You and your roommate may have been close within that apartment but now that you live apart, how is it different?

Take some time to acknowledge where you are with your friendships, and where you'd like to see your friendships go in this season. Use the space below along with the writing prompts to help you bring up some honest feelings, so you can align yourself with the right people.

1. Are you looking for something more substantial and meaningful?

   _____

2. How do you want to feel in a friendship? _____

   _____

3. How do you NOT want to feel? _____

_____

_____

4. What types of things do you want to do with friends right now?

_____

_____

5. What are five core values that are non-negotiable in a friendship?

_____

_____

6. What are your deal-breakers? _____

_____

_____

It's so hard to say goodbye to yesterday

When you say goodbye, you're also losing what the friendship *represented*. You're saying goodbye to a meaningful time period in your life. There's the friend you grew up with, the college friend, your colleague-turned-best-friend, the friend when you were single, the one that helped you through your breakup, and the bestie that you partied with for years. It's comforting to hold on to someone because you don't want to let go of that special time that connected you both.

It's time to figure out the true meaning of the actual friendship versus the time-period you don't want to say goodbye to.

"Giving up isn't the same as moving on."
—Marie Forleo

We feel there should be this big drawn-out discussion or fight. A final event to close the book. For me, what made certain endings hard was that there were no dramatic endings. The friendships simply faded. No one slept with my husband or betrayed me; we just grew apart because the effort and work weren't there. It's not that I don't care about these friends anymore, or that I don't miss them; it's quite the opposite.

I do miss them.
I will always love them.
Each one had a specific purpose in my life.

What helps me continue to heal is acknowledging all the gifts that these friendships gave me. Even the challenging ones were learning experiences, creating the person I am today and what I look for in a friendship. I honor the purpose of each friendship and how far I've come because of them. To me, friendships are never a waste of time. They are a gift no matter what the outcome.

Momline dating

How was I going meet new friends or how I was going to do it? How did women meet other women? Was it like online dating? Should I just cling on to my best friend down the street praying she'll introduce me to some of her friends? I slowly became more lost than I already was.

Online seemed to be the best option to meet other moms. I joined some Facebook groups; I went on MeetUp and searched anything involving new moms where I began to interact. With each event or play date that I'd attend, there would be very nice moms that I'd meet, but I found myself saying the familiar "eh."

I had responded to a play date from a Facebook group that was at mom's home. After I left the play date, I sat in my car with Brooklyn, drove about a block, parked the car, and just sobbed. Not only was I extremely lonely but at the same time, I was also putting in so much work to find new friends. With zero results.

Finding mom friends was pretty much in line with my dating experiences. Doing the research, narrowing it down, communicating, setting a date, showing up (hopefully they show up too), being disappointed within five minutes, and then starting all over again. It's exhausting. You can't help but ask yourself, "Is this what's out there? Is there ANY hope?!" Couldn't I just stay on my deserted island, see my old friends occasionally, and call it a day?

My husband had the best response when I returned in tears from the play date, "Baby, you're not going to be best friends with every woman you meet." This took me back to my mom's advice when I was online dating before my husband, "Honey, you can't look at every date as your future husband. Just enjoy the process and learn as much as you can."

The "click"

I wasn't getting that "click" that happens when you meet someone. If you aren't familiar with this "click," start paying attention when you meet someone and interact with her. The "click" doesn't happen often, but when it does, you'll know.

Trust the initial feeling when you meet a potential mom friend and how that feeling changes throughout your interaction with her. Yes, sometimes that feeling can be wrong. But most of that time that feeling is spot on. Use this feeling to be selective and intentional with your friendships. You don't have time to waste, and you deserve that quality friendship.

You aren't meant to do this alone

Historically and culturally, there was a strong community surrounding a new mother. Families used to live closer; sometimes grandma even lived with you. Other cultures place emphasis on the new mother's healing with everyone rallying around her. Then comes the good ol' USofA.

The reality is we are very lonely as new mothers, and even as our children grow older. The trap that I fell into is not only was I lonely, but I was also creating this huge isolation around me that just brought my loneliness to a whole other level. I'm sure I put out energy that the "kitchen is closed" where eventually people stop reaching out or offering.

It was a double-edged sword: I missed people dearly and wanted to make new friends, but at the same time, I just wanted to be left alone and not shower. I didn't want to be "on" because I was so exhausted and just not up to getting all dolled up to get drinks. There was insecurity in all areas of my life, down to what I could even handle as a mother. I didn't want people to see that. As a result, my world became smaller and smaller. I was stranded on a deserted island with no plan of how to escape.

We need community around us. We need it for: growth, happiness, connection, support, learning, mental health, gratitude, joy, strength, confidence, empathy, and trust. If you do not have a community of amazing women around you, go out there and create it yourself.

"Start before you're ready."

—Steven Pressfield

"I'm not ready."
"Maybe this isn't the right time."
"I don't feel like I'm in a place to meet someone new."
Or the worst one, "I don't need new friends."

That voice needs to be shut down, and you need to get out there. Today is the day you're going to do something that has risk but will create the courage inside you to take the next step. So many outside voices are telling us to get uncomfortable and get out of our comfort zones to grow. This goes for friendships too.

Your new friendship circle is entirely in your control but to create that circle, you have to stop hiding and hoping. Take action. One small step. Show up to a MOPS event. See what your church offers for new moms. Research groups at your hospital. Find therapists that may have group sessions that you can join. Stand on a corner and whistle at moms with their strollers; it doesn't matter!

Real, raw, and relatable

I'll keep this part short, sweet, and to the point. To create and *maintain* friendships, you must be vulnerable. We are seeing this everywhere, from Brené Brown to Jessica Honegger to Jen Hatmaker, and their messages about the bravery behind vulnerability. It's essential in relationships. This goes for making, and keeping, those mom friends you need to survive. Being vulnerable allows you to be:

- Relatable
- Authentic
- Warm
- Inviting
- Interesting

We all know the perfect mom who doesn't poop, fart, her kids are always good, her marriage never has issues, she never has a complaint, and she rarely contributes her story when you're all talking about something challenging. Unfortunately, no matter how sweet she is and how much she helps you when you're in a pinch, she is seen as:

- Boring
- Unapproachable
- Distant
- Judgmental
- Insecure

Now which feelings would make you want to make time and effort to make and maintain a long-lasting friendship? Which person would you look forward to seeing the next time so she can continue telling her story? I love this quote from Bob Marley, and it really validates the importance of being vulnerable to create and cultivate your friendships:

"You find that being vulnerable is the only way to allow your heart to feel true pleasure that's so real it scares you. You find strength in knowing you have a true friend and possibly a soul mate who will remain loyal to the end."

Do yourself a favor, with the next potential mom friends you make: Be real. Be honest. Be relatable. Everybody's kids have meltdowns. Everyone is behind. No one knows what the hell they are doing. We're all in this together.

Anyone that judges you or turns their nose up at the story about your boobs leaking in line at Starbucks is not a friend for you. The friend for you is the one that laughs and either says, "OMG that happened to me at Target!" or "That sounds like something that WOULD happen to me at Target!" Don't invest in women who are emotionally constipated. Everybody poops. Everybody farts. Keep it real.

"Making a friend and maintaining a friendship are two different things."
—Sonya Teclai, poet and musician

Making new friends is hard the older we get. Keeping and maintaining friendships is even harder. Add these to the big list of "to dos" we are keeping inside our heads, and you can get overwhelmed about where your life is headed. Wondering who will be there right by your side.

You have to be a relatable woman if you want to meet relatable women who "get you." The only way to do that is jump in, meet people, and be open to disappointment along with surprise. Take chances, try new experiences, go to play dates, join a mommy-and-me music group (and find a mom who will roll her eyes with you), find a new-mom support group, a healthy Facebook group, or even enroll your child in some type of early childhood school where you can meet some new moms in the same boat as you.

When you find the friends that are right for you, cherish them and do whatever it takes to give life to that friendship. Focus your efforts here, not the friend who can't even respond to a text message you sent her weeks ago. That friend isn't a horrible person; she's just not in your season, and for some reason she's not making time for you. You'll become exhausted, frustrated, and eventually sad with nothing helping you get through that.

When you can find mom friends that want to make the time for you, can share similar stories, challenges, complaints, bring some laughs, and you are able to do similar things together, it's just so much easier and natural.

Just keep in your back pocket

1. Now that you're a mother, for your friendships to survive, they need cultivation.

2. Have patience with not only yourself, but also the time it will take to connect with women you're meeting. It takes time and work to build that to an actual friendship. Even more time to maintain and make it stronger.

3. Take risks. Take chances. Walk away with zero regrets.

4. You won't connect with everyone, and everyone won't connect with you. That's normal.

5. Check in on your expectations of the friendship and if they match with theirs.

6. Know when to say goodbye.

7. Never chase a friendship. Or any relationship for that matter.

8. Be friendly and say hello to a mom you walk by. If you see a mom with a baby at the library, strike up some small talk, and see if it can get deeper. If you notice a mom struggling at the grocery store, ask if she needs help and give her something to smile about. You know how nice that would have been on your toughest days.

"Remember, you don't need a certain number of friends, just a number of friends you can be certain of"

—Unknown

It's time to be intentional with finding friends as well. No need for casual acquaintances anymore. You don't have enough time, and you need to make time for the right people. Throughout the last ten years, I've gathered a hearty handful of true friends that simply fill the palm of that hand. I don't need to count my friends on my fingers like I used to. I'm very selective on whom I hold close to my heart and whom I make time and effort to paint the town red, yellow, green, and every other color in the rainbow.

CHAPTER 10

Social Media is the
New Supermodel

"Your life can only be as fulfilling as your interpretation of your experience. Your perception. No matter how great, if you don't have a healthy relationship to those experiences, then no matter what amazing things happen, you're not going to feel fulfilled." —Julianna Raye

I didn't know how to enjoy the beauty of the photograph and associate it with entertainment. Instead, the pages I flipped through became the standard on how I should look and a reminder of the lifestyle I should, but wasn't, living. I never thought about the camera angles, clothing techniques, airbrushing, or weeks of nutritional deprivation that created the photo in front of me. A model that was perhaps internally miserable, forcing every smile and pose. As a teenager and college student, I mindlessly traveled through the glossy pages of *Vogue, Cosmopolitan,* and *Vanity Fair.* I paused and stared at the model who defined glamour, beauty, and excitement. I felt like I knew her entire life, but the reality was I didn't know her at all.

A spark that creates connection

When Brooklyn was born, she became a huge part of my social media. My postings began on the day she was born, and from that day forward, everything about her was random, funny, and oh-so-adorable. Things like her first fart, an accidental Elvis smile (probably while farting), when she discovered and stared at her fist for the first time, how she was *obsessed* with staring at ceiling fans, and me up at 4 a.m. and asking if anyone else was.

Facebook "friends" I barely knew would stop me at a local parade or around town and ask, "Are you Brooklyn?" where we would stop to chat with the fan that Brooklyn created. I didn't think it was creepy, nor did I ever feel the person stopping me was going to kidnap Brooklyn. What I felt and saw was pure joy and a person that was brave enough to introduce themselves and tell me how happy my posts were making them. The bonus was, I had officially met my Facebook "friend" and created a connection beyond our phones. After all, that's what social media is all about, right?

What a mom wants,
what a mom needs

I'll say it again, motherhood can be lonely. If you're like me, you may be trapped inside while your body heals or until you're comfortable leaving your house. Obviously we crave *some* kind of connection if we aren't getting the live stuff. Social media is perfect for this.

Sometimes I want to burn social media at the stake. However, there have been some awesome things that have happened to me because of it. Not only have I met amazing women, but I've also learned a lot when it comes to raising my daughter. I was a part of fabulous mommy Facebook groups that were the support I needed at the time and didn't require me to leave my front door. I also virtually kept myself connected to friends and family that I couldn't physically see. Human beings crave and need connection; I don't care what you tell yourself. Social media can help you with this connection while you adjust to this new life of yours. Until you're ready to "go live."

Baby steps

Half the battle is admitting motherhood can be boring. The other half is what can you do about it? The solution is so simple but also one of our biggest challenges: finding others to connect with. At least then you can have someone to talk to about how boring motherhood can be!

In the beginning, you may not be ready to leave the house and meet new friends. It can be kind of scary if you haven't done it in a while too. Or maybe you're ready to rip the king-size pad off, get those yoga pants back on, and bust the hell out of your house? Everyone is different. If you're like how I was, I just wasn't ready to leave my house those first few months. I thought I had all the friends I needed (although I wasn't seeing any of them) and was nervous meeting new people. Luckily there was a way for me to find the connection I was so desperate for.

Social media was the way for me to slowly connect with moms in the same season I was in. I also found moms that were in a different stage, but still weathering the motherhood storm and open to making friends. My connection began with 2 a.m. desperate pleas of help with anything from breastfeeding, sleep, first foods, weaning, teething, and safe products for Brooklyn. I found women and groups that lived near me. Eventually when I was ready to get some air and venture out into the world, these groups had ways to meet face-to-face.

I encourage you to join just one. Search for groups in your town or ask a friend if she knows of any that are worth joining. Take your time getting to know these moms, and eventually, you'll have the confidence and comfort to meet them in person. Maybe even make a life-long friend.

Keep an eye out for ...

Finding mom friends on social media is pretty much like starting any relationship. There will be some red flags to watch out for and pay attention to. When you do join a Facebook group or form relationships within Instagram, remember what you've always looked for in a friendship and honor that even with meeting moms on social media. Look for women who make you feel:

- *Accepted.* They open their arms to you and make you feel welcomed.

- *Respected.* They give advice without judgement; they acknowledge your feelings and are empathetic.

- *Appreciated.* They make you feel important and valued.

Down the rabbit hole

Anything can have a dark side. I finally admitted to myself that I was way too connected and addicted to social media. I'd create a post and obsessively check the responses throughout the day. There would be a heated discussion within a mommy Facebook group where I felt free to give my commentary, only to have my heart race and anger elevate with each comment I'd read and respond to. I would then obsessively check the post throughout the day. How many hearts did my photo of Brooklyn and I eating ice cream get? Why didn't anyone comment or answer the question I asked in my post? How many views did my Instagram story get? How many followers did I have?

Quiet moments and boredom throughout the day prompted my fingers to pick up my phone and check for updates on Instagram. Brooklyn played in the corner, putting blocks in her mouth, while I found it impossible to stop scrolling Facebook. There were times when I'd say to myself out loud, "Michelle, PUT DOWN THE PHONE!"

I would get so mad at myself. I knew I had a problem. Social media was even affecting my mood and how I reacted to my family.

Social media is a wonderful way to find connection. But like anything, too much is never a good thing. As moms, we can find ourselves mindlessly scrolling as our baby nurses or sleeps all day. We can become emotionally affected by what we read. It can consume us.

Why are you using social media anyways?

- Is it bringing you joy?
- Are you learning?
- Connecting with other awesome moms and resources?
- Is it giving you the opportunity to share moments with family?
- Does it bring you laughter?
- Do you get helpful tips, tricks, and hacks on raising your children?
- Is it impossible to leave your house right now where you love the connection you have with other moms on a Facebook group?

If you answered YES to 80 percent of these, you're seeing the benefits that social media can bring to you. On the other hand,

- Do you use it as an escape?
- When you're stressed, do you grab the phone and find comfort?
- When you're bored, is it the first thing you think of to do?
- When you hear an alert, is it difficult not to look at your phone?
- Are you up until midnight scrolling without intention?
- Is social media making you sad? Insecure? Angry?

Same deal here, if you answered YES to most of these, it's time to evaluate what is going on and make some changes. This chapter will help you do that.

What's helped me manage my connection to social media

1. If I post something, I do it in the morning and don't check the feed until evening. You need to decide why you're posting something. Is it to share with family and friends, or is it to see how many people will react to it? When you post to simply share, you don't need to check the status every ten minutes.

2. If you find you scroll when you're bored, try to find other things to do when you're bored or have some downtime. Make a habit of picking up a book or listening to a podcast. Take a walk. Call your mom. Get coffee with a friend.

3. Put your phone in a place that isn't easily accessible. At night, enjoy time with your partner and leave your phone downstairs. If you use your phone as an alarm, buy a $3 alarm clock at Walmart.

4. Schedule social media in your day and honor those time slots. Set goals of how long you want to be on social media each day and check in on your usage to see if you're on track.

Disconnection brings you connection

I ripped the Band-Aid off. For the entire month of December, I took a social media break.

How did I do? It was challenging but from December 1st to January 4th, I didn't log on ONCE. I deleted my Facebook and Instagram apps. There were times I had to tell myself out loud not to go on. I had to find other things to occupy the quiet moments. I would put my phone upstairs when I was downstairs. I'd leave it downstairs when I laid my head on my pillow. As hard as it was in the beginning, like most things, it got easier the longer I did it.

How was the break? Incredible. I felt so connected to my friends, I was more present with my family, more creative with my time, and made more effort to physically be with people. Brooklyn had two weeks off school and when we did our little excursions, I interacted with her more and paid attention to the moment versus constantly taking photos. The holidays had me enjoying every moment in live form versus looking for those perfect opportunities to post something.

To be honest, initially, I didn't look forward to returning to social media. I was nervous I'd go back to my old habits and feelings. I enjoyed the freedom. But alas, I returned!

Will I do it again? Absolutely. Do I fall into my old patterns at times? Of course. But I believe this detox has now given me the awareness to check in on myself, my social media health, and connect in other ways than social media. The perfect cocktail.

Staying present versus creating a documentary

I questioned why I felt the need to document every moment of my daughter's life, a vacation, or dinner with friends on my phone. I was curious if I was alone and spent time observing other behaviors with their phone. Even though it was upsetting to see how much parents were on their phone, I knew I was in that same boat doing the exact same thing.

By the time Brooklyn turned three, I had tens of thousands of photos and videos of Brooklyn. I haven't gone through some of them in years and forget what's even on my hard drive. If it was her birthday party, my husband and I would be on our phone the entire party documenting it. I was missing the party and connection with my daughter. Looking into a phone versus into her eyes.

There's nothing wrong with wanting to capture milestone moments and hilarious footage of your children, but next time you're with your family, maybe one of you can be the ringleader of the photos. Instead of twenty photos, take a couple good ones and just sit back and watch her open her presents. Try to have one day where you don't take any photos at all and just be with one another.

Waitress?
I'll have what she's having

Human beings also have the need to feel SIGNIFICANT in this world and to be noticed. Unfortunately, at times we measure our significance based on the attention and approval of others. As a mom, you may find a growing desire to be unique during a time when you feel the most boring. You may believe that now that you're a mom, you have nothing to show for other than sore nipples and a greasy top knot. A photo of a mother with a dusty filter, gorgeous locks (even if they are extensions), peaceful twins in matching outfits, and a hundred "likes" may have you thinking, "What can I do to stand out like her?"

Our need for significance in this world shows its ugly little head in the form of comparison. We're rarely comparing to become better; we're comparing and feeling like shit about ourselves. Yes, there are times when I'm scrolling, reading, or observing other women, and I'm inspired to learn, do better, and be better. I do believe that inspiration comes from the outside as well as what's internal. But let's be real.

When it comes to being a mom, we're judging, falling down a rabbit hole, or getting dark about where someone else is compared to where we are in that moment. When you're scrolling through Instagram at 9 p.m. after a long day of the un-glamorous world of mom-shit, are you getting a burst to do better or be better? Or is it more like a two-hour trap of internally ripping on whoever you're following, what they look like, but at the same time feeling you should be doing what they're doing? Are you filled with regret, panic about what you're missing, and all the things you need to change to be as colorful as your feed?

Apples to oranges

I believe it's only natural and healthy to compare ourselves from time to time. It allows for us to "check in" on our own selves and if we are truly happy where we are in life. But are you comparing their best ... to your worst?

The personal development junkie inside of me is constantly reading books, blogs, newsletters, watching videos, taking courses, following influencers, and ingesting ways for me to be the "best version" of myself. With all the information and inspiration that is out there, it's easy for me to get clouded with everyone else's story and not connect with what will work for me as a unique individual. It's easy to be intrigued by what someone else is doing, especially when it's something so pretty, put together, and gets attention.

I'll break it to you gently, that person you're staring at and comparing yourself to is a human just like you. The story you're creating in your mind, what you feel you should live up to, is someone else's. When we are lost with who we are as unique individuals, we search for the answers in others. Take a moment to acknowledge where YOU are at right now and if you're on shaky ground in this mom role. Put the book down for five minutes and discover if there are any doubts about your confidence, connection to your needs, and love for yourself in this new life you're in. If the ground is too shaky right now, you may have to assess if this is the best time to be on social media.

Just remember

Social media has become a bragging platform for many. The perfect picture moments along with the staged imperfections have created this unofficial competition amongst moms. Remember this as you look at a post, and don't forget the other parts of their day that are too real to share on their feeds.

Comparison puts the emphasis and work on the wrong person

Do not be a fraud. The more you live another person's life, dreams, and goals, the further you are from yours. Comparison grows when you lose focus on what fulfills you. When you connect with your own goals and intention— comparison diminishes.

It's time to figure out YOUR strengths, YOUR values and what YOU offer as a woman and mother. If you can't answer any of these, this is your time to use whatever tools to help you navigate toward finding the answers. Podcasts, books, writing, workshops, finding women that you can relate to, walks in nature (this is when my brain really gets going), trying new things, and be honest about what truly makes YOU happy. It's work, and you must do the work to find who you are—and honor it. Then you can scroll without falling into comparison.

Some daily rituals for you

- Instead of comparing yourself to other people, create the habit of comparing to *yourself.* See how much *you* have grown, what *you* have achieved, and what progress *you* have made toward *your* goals.

- Be in tune with your feelings with whom you follow. If you don't get all the good feels when you see someone on your feed, or you fall into the comparison trap, it is time let go. Make space for those that inspire you, bring you joy, and you learn best from.

- Work hard to grow spiritually, physically, and emotionally. Commit to growing every day, so your confidence in your unique life will shield you from the comparison trap.

- Actively stop, pause, and create gratitude, appreciation, and kindness toward yourself.

- Put the phone down and be present with how far you have come, the challenges you've overcome, and all the good things you are giving and doing for others around you.

- What traits and talents about yourself do you appreciate? What do you love about yourself? If you had five minutes to brag about yourself, what would you say?

The perfect cocktail

You deserve to scroll through a social media feed and find the photos that bring you joy. You should be exposed to posts that are learning opportunities and you want to share them with your best friends. You can post something with the simple intention of bringing joy to whoever sees it. You can look at a photo and appreciate its beauty instead of feeling your life is lacking.

After you figure out how to make social media work for you, the second part is how you can make it work for other mothers. Cheer them on, as you'd want to be cheered. Virtually hug other mothers, as you need that hug too. Get in that darn rocky boat with her and tell her you're in this storm with her. Help her without shaming her. Don't contribute to cruel comments, instead put those fires out.

Motherhood is a mixture of many emotions, insecurities, doubts, and fear which creates the ultimate social media hangover. Like anything in life, social media can turn ugly if used and interpreted in the wrong ways. The good news is you now have some tools to help you use social media in ways to support you through motherhood. It may take some time and hard work, but you'll get there.

CONCLUSION

You are an incredible mother
You are doing the best that you can
Motherhood is the biggest life change you'll make
What you are feeling is real
It is the truth
Do not ignore your feelings
It can be scary
But you're not alone
You have me
It's time to acknowledge your feelings
Break free from expectations
And live the life you're meant to live

With Love,
Michelle

ACKNOWLEDGEMENTS

I could not have done this without my husband Bobby's support. He may have been a silent partner through the ride, but whenever I needed him, he was right there cheering me on. Maybe he doubted this book would ever happen, and I don't blame him, but he never led me to believe this. I love him more than I let him know.

My mom. For always wanting to know "how is the book going?" or to simply just be by my side throughout this motherhood journey.

To all my incredible friends. Even the ones I've lost. You've all supported me, encouraged me, and have been the first ones waiting for this book to be born.

To my developmental editor, Jen Lien. Our year-long marriage of creating this book, your incredibly hard work, suggestions, revisions, all I learned and how I became a better writer because of you.

To Rea Fry and Joe Tower of WriteWay. Thank you for taking me through the grueling book proposal process. For educating me on so much about this publishing world. For believing in the book. You gave me permission to trust my voice and use it. The support you've given me, the pitching, the suggestions, the connections; I cannot imagine my life and this book without you. Thank you, Rea, for trusting me enough to introduce me to Rachel.

Rachel Beck, my agent who also believed in this mission. Who listened to why I wanted this book in the world and why it was needed. You took dozens of chances sharing my book proposal to publishers. I didn't want to give up because of you.

To the listeners of *The Honest Mom Podcast*. I appreciate each of you bringing me to your ears and hearts. You all inspired me to get this book out to the world to walk alongside the podcast.

ABOUT MICHELLE

Michelle Mansfield is a podcaster, author, health coach, and most importantly, mother. She is also a fitness and yoga instructor, loves nature walks, crystals, reiki, drawing cards of any kind, music, girls' night with Brooklyn (every Thursday!), and being surrounded by her incredible friends.

With her writing, she healed and hopes to help others see that being vulnerable isn't a weakness. It's the first step to their own healing. *The Honest Mom Podcast* was born when Michelle knew her voice was something that busy and exhausted moms would appreciate. Her passion for wellness in all areas of living has been the driving force to bring all she's learned into every mother's hands. *The Honest Mom Project* is her first "grown-up" book which initially was a diary for her own healing.

Michelle is also a children's author of the *Brooklyn Wellness Series* (www.itsjustmebrooklyn.com) showcasing her daughter, Brooklyn, through wellness themes such as confidence, independence, being adventurous with new foods, and walking alongside one's fears.

You can connect with Michelle on her website,
www.michellemansfieldauthor.com

THE
Honest Mom
PODCAST

WITH MICHELLE MANSFIELD

Start listening to *The Honest Mom Podcast* today
by scanning the QR code below: